Master the Wood Pellet Grill & Smoker COOKBOOK

Recipes to Improve Your Smoking Today

By

Eli Turner

Scan the QR code to sign up for our newsletter.

TABLE OF CONTENTS

RECIPES

Dedication

To my loving wife and our incredible children,

Your unwavering support and boundless love inspire me. This book is as much a reflection of our shared journey as it is of my passion for cooking. Thank you for being my greatest taste-testers, supporters, and the heart of my life.

With all my love,

Eli

About the Author

Eli Turner is a master chef in the art of pellet grilling. With a career spanning over twenty years, Eli has perfected smoking meats and transformed each meal into a smoky masterpiece. His passion for the deep, rich flavors that only a pellet grill can achieve has earned him a loyal following among food enthusiasts and home cooks.

Married to his high school sweetheart, Eli is a dedicated family man with two wonderful children. His family serves as his greatest support, often acting as the first taste testers for his culinary creations. Eli's home is a hub of delicious aromas and hearty laughter, where food brings everyone together.

Eli's expertise with the pellet grill is not just about cooking; it's about creating unforgettable experiences. Whether he's hosting a weekend barbecue or teaching a masterclass on smoking techniques, Eli Turner brings his signature blend of skill, creativity, and love for family to every dish he prepares.

Chapter 1:

Introduction

Pellet grills have revolutionized the world of outdoor cooking, offering BBQ lovers a versatile and convenient way to create delicious, smoky dishes with minimal effort. As a fusion of traditional grilling and modern technology, pellet grills have gained immense popularity among barbecue and cooking enthusiasts.

At the heart of a pellet grill lies its innovative design, which utilizes hardwood pellets as the primary fuel source. These pellets, made from compressed sawdust or wood chips, are carefully designed to provide rich, smoky flavors to food while providing consistent heat and temperature control throughout the cooking process.

Unlike traditional charcoal or gas grills, pellet grills operate using an automated system that regulates airflow and fuel delivery, ensuring precise temperature control with minimal manual intervention. This advanced technology allows users to set their desired temperature and indulge in their other chores without worrying about the food, as they know that their food will be cooked to perfection every time.

One of the key features that set pellet grills apart is their versatility. Whether you're smoking brisket low and slow, preparing steaks to perfection, or baking mouthwatering desserts, a pellet grill offers the flexibility to easily handle a wide range of cooking techniques. With adjustable temperature settings and customizable smoke levels, users can customize their cooking experience to achieve the desired flavor profile for each dish.

Furthermore, pellet grills are designed with convenience in mind. Many models come with digital controls, allowing users to remotely monitor and adjust cooking temperatures using smartphones or tablets. Imagine the convenience of setting your desired temperature with the turn of a dial or the tap of a touchscreen, then stepping back to let the grill work its magic. With a pellet grill, this dream becomes a reality. This level of convenience makes pellet grills an ideal choice for busy individuals who want to enjoy barbecue without being tied to the grill.

In addition to their practicality and versatility, pellet grills are also known for being eco-friendly. By using renewable wood pellets as fuel, these grills produce minimal emissions and leave behind little to no ash, making them a sustainable option for environmentally conscious cooks.

Why Pellet Grills are Essential for an Ideal BBQ?

Few tools are as indispensable as the pellet grill in outdoor cooking. Revered for their versatility, precision, and unparalleled flavor infusion, pellet grills are nowadays considered the foundations of the barbecue experience, transforming backyard gatherings into unforgettable feasts.

Pellet grills' unique design and functionality are at the heart of the matter. Unlike charcoal or gas-operated devices, which rely on inconsistent heat sources and manual intervention, pellet grills utilize the power of advanced technology to deliver consistent, reliable results with minimal effort.

Introduction

One key advantage of pellet grills is their ability to maintain precise temperature control throughout the cooking process. Their automated auger system and digital temperature controls offer unmatched accuracy, ensuring your food cooks evenly and retain its natural juices and flavors. This level of precision is essential for achieving the ideal barbecue experience, allowing you to enjoy perfectly cooked meats.

Moreover, pellet grills are versatile, offering various cooking options to suit every taste and preference. Whether you're craving tender, slow-smoked ribs, grilled chicken, or perfectly seared steaks, a pellet grill provides the flexibility to easily manage every situation. This versatility is essential for creating a well-rounded barbecue menu that caters to your guests' diverse tastes and ensures that everyone leaves the table satisfied.

Another compelling reason pellet grills are essential for an ideal barbecue is their unparalleled flavor infusion capabilities. By using hardwood pellets as the primary fuel source, pellet grills impart a rich, smoky flavor to food that cannot be replicated with other cooking methods. This also allows you to customize your barbecue experience to suit your personal taste preferences.

Furthermore, pellet grills offer unmatched convenience, making them indispensable for busy cooks who want to enjoy barbecue without being tied to the grill. With features such as Wi-Fi connectivity and smartphone integration, you can monitor and adjust your grill settings from anywhere, allowing you to multitask, socialize, or simply relax while your food cooks to perfection. This level of convenience is essential for modern cooks who value their time and seek convenient solutions for their culinary experiences.

To conclude, the importance of pellet grills in achieving an ideal barbecue cannot be underestimated. From their precise temperature control and versatile cooking options to their unparalleled flavor infusion capabilities and unmatched convenience, pellet grills transform the outdoor cooking experience into an enjoyable activity. Therefore, do not hesitate to invest in a pellet grill. Trust me, this decision will elevate your barbecue game to new heights and ensure that every cooking experience is a success.

Why you Must Consider a Pellet Grill for your Memorable BBQ Experiences

While countless options are available for barbecue lovers and backyard barbecue enthusiasts, the unique combination of features and benefits offered by pellet grills makes them an undeniable choice for anyone seeking to elevate their BBQ experiences to new heights.

First and foremost, the precision and consistency provided by pellet grills set them apart from other outdoor cooking methods. Unlike traditional charcoal or gas grills, which can be prone to fluctuations in temperature and uneven heat distribution, pellet grills utilize advanced technology to maintain steady, reliable cooking conditions throughout the cooking period. This level of control is crucial for achieving perfectly cooked, tender, and juicy meats.

Furthermore, the versatility of pellet grills cannot be underestimated. Whether you're hosting a casual backyard BBQ party, a festive gathering with friends and family, or a formal dinner party, a pellet grill offers the flexibility to cater to any occasion and culinary preference. From low and slow smoking to high-temperature grilling and everything in between, pellet grills empower you to explore various cooking techniques and recipes.

Apart from the above reasons, perhaps the most compelling reason to consider a pellet grill for your memorable BBQ experiences is the unparalleled flavor infusion it provides. Using hardwood pellets as fuel, pellet grills impart a rich, smoky essence to your food that cannot be replicated with other cooking methods.

In addition to their barbecuing benefits, pellet grills offer practical benefits, making them a sound investment for any outdoor cooking enthusiast. Features such as digital temperature controls, Wi-Fi connectivity, and easy-to-clean designs enhance the user experience.

Finally, it's worth noting that pellet grills are not just a tool for cooking; they're a gateway to a lifestyle centered around good food, great company, and the joy of outdoor living. Believe me, you will not regret investing in a pellet grill. In fact, considering a pellet grill for your memorable BBQ experiences will enhance your outdoor cooking adventures in ways you never thought possible. With their precision, versatility, flavor infusion capabilities, and practical benefits, pellet grills offer everything you need to elevate your BBQ game and create lasting memories that will be relished for years.

Chapter 2:

Benefits of Pellet Grill

Barbecuing is a rich and diverse experience of flavor, tradition, and community and pallet grill is at the center of this wonderful experience. It's a revolutionary tool that has forever changed the landscape of BBQ and elevated the experience of new and seasoned chefs.

Learning about the core elements that set pellet grills apart from others is essential to understanding their significant impacts on your BBQ experience. From their innovative design and advanced technology to their unparalleled flavor infusion capabilities and practical benefits, pellet grills have reshaped how we approach outdoor cooking.

One of the most significant impacts of pellet grills on your BBQ experience is their ability to deliver consistent, reliable results with minimal effort. Unlike traditional charcoal or gas grills, which require constant monitoring and adjustment to maintain steady cooking conditions, pellet grills utilize automated systems and precise temperature controls to ensure that your food cooks evenly and perfectly every time. This level of consistency is essential for achieving the ideal BBQ experience.

Another significant impact of pellet grills on your BBQ experience is their ability to impart rich, smoky flavors to your food that cannot be replicated with other cooking methods. By using hardwood pellets as the primary fuel source, pellet grills infuse your meats with a depth of flavor that tantalizes the taste buds and leaves a lasting impression on all who indulge.

In addition to their flavor infusion capabilities, pellet grills offer practical benefits that enhance the overall BBQ experience. Features like digital temperature controls, Wi-Fi connectivity, and easy-to-clean designs streamline the cooking process and allow you to focus on what matters most, creating unforgettable memories with loved ones around the grill. Furthermore, pellet grills are environmentally friendly, using renewable wood pellets as fuel and producing minimal emissions and ash, making them a sustainable choice for eco-conscious consumers.

Benefits of Pellet Grills

Following are some of the most significant benefits of pellet grills.

It Makes Barbecuing Easy

One of the primary benefits of pellet grills is that they simplify the art of barbecuing. Their innovative design and functionality of pellet grills make barbecuing easy and enjoyable. Unlike charcoal grills, which require extreme attention to lighting and temperature control, or gas grills, which can be prone to flare-ups and uneven heating, pellet grills operate using a straightforward and intuitive system that simplifies barbecuing.

Their automated temperature control mechanism is central to the ease of use of pellet grills. Equipped with digital controllers and precision auger systems, pellet grills allow users to set their desired cooking temperature with a button, eliminating the need for constant monitoring and adjustment. This convenience level means you can simply load your grill with pellets, set your desired temperature, and let the grill do the rest.

Furthermore, pellet grills offer unparalleled consistency in cooking results, ensuring that your meats are cooked evenly. By maintaining a steady temperature throughout the cooking process, pellet grills eliminate the risk of overcooking or undercooking your food, allowing you to achieve consistent and delicious results with minimal effort.

In short, pellet grills' ability to make barbecuing easy is a game-changer for outdoor cooking enthusiasts everywhere. With their intuitive design, automated temperature control, and versatile cooking capabilities, pellet grills offer a hassle-free approach to barbecuing that allows cooks of all skill levels to achieve delicious results with minimal effort.

It Makes the Cooking Experience Enjoyable

Cooking with a pellet grill not only simplifies the process but also enhances the overall enjoyment of the culinary experience, transforming it into a delightful and rewarding task. With their user-friendly design, versatile cooking capabilities, and ability to infuse rich, smoky flavors into every dish, pellet grills offer a truly immersive cooking experience that captivates the senses and brings joy to cooks of all skill levels.

One of the primary ways pellet grills make the cooking experience enjoyable is through their intuitive design and ease of use. Unlike traditional barbecue methods, which require constant monitoring and adjustment, pellet grills streamline the cooking process, allowing users to set their desired temperature and let the grill rest. This hands-off approach frees cooks from the constraints of the kitchen, enabling them to relax, socialize, or simply enjoy the outdoor ambiance while their food cooks to perfection.

Furthermore, pellet grills are designed with user convenience and comfort in mind, ensuring that every aspect of the cooking experience is enjoyable and stress-free. Many models come equipped with easy-to-read digital displays, ergonomic controls, and spacious cooking surfaces, allowing cooks to focus on the joy of cooking without worrying about the technical details. Additionally, pellet grills are often built with durable materials and innovative technology, ensuring reliable performance and long-lasting enjoyment for years.

They are Safe to Handle

One of the primary concerns in any cooking experience is safety and pellet grills excel in providing a secure and worry-free environment for cooks of all levels. With their thoughtful design features, built-in safety mechanisms, and user-friendly operation, pellet grills offer peace of mind and confidence, allowing chefs to focus on the culinary task without compromising safety.

One of the primary ways pellet grills ensure safety is through their enclosed cooking chambers and insulated construction. Unlike traditional charcoal grills, which can pose a fire hazard due to open flames and hot coals, pellet grills feature sealed cooking compartments that contain heat and prevent flare-ups. This design minimizes the risk of accidental burns and injuries. It reduces the likelihood of outdoor fires, making pellet grills a safe and responsible choice for outdoor cooking.

Moreover, pellet grills have built-in safety features that enhance reliability and security. From automatic shutdown mechanisms that activate in the event of a malfunction to temperature sensors and alarms that alert users to potential hazards, pellet grills are designed with the utmost consideration for user safety. These features provide a layer of protection and reassurance, giving cooks the confidence to cook with peace of mind, knowing that their grill is equipped to handle any situation.

Additionally, pellet grills are engineered with user convenience and comfort in mind, ensuring that every aspect of the cooking experience is safe and enjoyable. Many models come equipped with ergonomic handles, sturdy legs, and stable bases, providing a stable and secure platform for cooking even in challenging outdoor environments. Furthermore, pellet grills often feature easy-to-use controls and intuitive interfaces, reducing the risk of user error and ensuring a smooth and hassle-free cooking experience.

Furthermore, using hardwood pellets as the primary fuel source in pellet grills offers cooks an additional layer of safety and peace of mind. Unlike traditional charcoal or propane grills, which can emit harmful chemicals and pollutants when burned, hardwood pellets are made from natural, renewable materials and produce minimal emissions and ash. This eco-friendly fuel source reduces the environmental impact of outdoor cooking. It ensures a clean and safe cooking environment for you and your loved ones.

They are Versatile Outdoor Cooking Machines

Pellet grills offer a level of versatility that goes beyond traditional barbecue methods. From smoking and grilling to roasting and baking, pellet grills serve as multi-functional outdoor cooking machines that empower users to explore a diverse range of cooking techniques and recipes.

Unlike conventional charcoal or gas grills, which are often limited in their cooking capabilities, pellet grills utilize an innovative system that combines precise temperature control with consistent heat distribution. This allows for a wide range of cooking options and possibilities, empowering chefs to experiment with new flavors, ingredients, and cooking methods easily.

One primary way pellet grills showcase their versatility is by smoking meats low and slow to perfection. Whether you are craving tender, fall-off-the-bone ribs or mouthwatering brisket, a pellet grill provides the ideal environment for achieving rich, smoky flavors and a melt-in-your-mouth texture that epitomizes classic barbecue fare. With adjustable temperature settings and customizable smoke levels, users can tailor their smoking experience to suit their preferences and create unforgettable culinary experiences.

In addition to smoking, pellet grills excel in their grilling capabilities, allowing users to easily achieve perfectly seared steaks, juicy burgers, and flavorful vegetables. By providing consistent heat and precise temperature control, pellet grills ensure even cooking and delicious results every time, whether you prefer rare, medium, or well-done meats.

Moreover, pellet grills are designed to accommodate various cooking accessories and attachments, enhancing their versatility and functionality. From grill grates and smoker boxes to pizza stones and rotisserie kits, pellet grills can be customized to suit your specific cooking needs and preferences, allowing you to expand your outdoor cooking repertoire and confidently tackle new challenges.

They are Safe for your Health and Environment

It is essential to consider not only the flavors and textures of the dishes we create but also the impact of our cooking methods on our health and the environment. In this regard, pellet grills stand out as a responsible choice for outdoor cooking, offering a safe and eco-friendly alternative to traditional barbecue methods that prioritize the well-being of both users and the environment.

One primary way pellet grills contribute to health and environmental safety is by using natural hardwood pellets as the primary fuel source. Unlike charcoal or gas grills, which can emit harmful chemicals and pollutants when burned, hardwood pellets are made from renewable wood sources and produce minimal emissions and ash when ignited. This eco-friendly fuel choice reduces air pollution and carbon emissions. It promotes sustainable practices, ensuring our outdoor cooking activities have minimal environmental impact.

Furthermore, the clean-burning nature of hardwood pellets makes pellet grills a healthier option for outdoor cooking, as they eliminate the risk of exposure to harmful chemicals and carcinogens that can be present in charcoal or propane fumes. Using natural, renewable fuels and producing minimal emissions, pellet grills provide a safer and more environmentally responsible cooking solution for users and their families, promoting a healthier and more sustainable lifestyle.

In addition to their environmental benefits, pellet grills offer practical advantages that contribute to health and safety in outdoor cooking. With their enclosed cooking chambers and insulated construction, pellet grills minimize the risk of flare-ups and outdoor fires, providing users a secure and worry-free cooking environment. This design reduces the likelihood of accidental burns and injuries. It ensures that cooking is controlled and responsible, minimizing the risk of damage to property and the surrounding environment.

They Impart the Best Flavor to Meat

One of the primary reasons pellet grills impart the best flavor to meat is their unique fuel source: hardwood pellets. Crafted from natural hardwoods, these pellets serve as the foundation of flavor in pellet grilling, imparting a depth and complexity that cannot be replicated with other cooking methods.

Moreover, pellet grills offer precise control over the smoking process, allowing users to tailor the intensity and duration of smoke exposure to achieve their desired flavor profile. Whether you prefer a subtle hint of smoke or a bold, robust smokiness, pellet grills can customize your smoking experience and create dishes that reflect your taste preferences.

Furthermore, the indirect heat generated by pellet grills promotes even cooking and moisture retention in meats, resulting in tender, juicy cuts that burst with flavor from the inside out. Unlike direct grilling methods, which can lead to dryness and uneven cooking, pellet grills provide a gentle and consistent heat that allows meats to cook slowly and evenly, preserving their natural juices and maximizing flavor absorption.

In addition to their flavor infusion capabilities, pellet grills offer practical benefits that contribute to their reputation as masters of taste. Features such as digital temperature controls, precise auger systems, and spacious cooking surfaces ensure that every grilling process is optimized for flavor excellence, allowing users to focus on their barbecue without worrying about technical details or inconsistencies.

Chapter 3:

How Do They Work?

Pellet grills have garnered considerable attention in recent years for their exceptional cooking capabilities and their positive environmental impact. As environmental concerns continue to rise and sustainability becomes an increasingly pressing issue, many outdoor cooking lovers are turning to pellet grills as a responsible choice that prioritizes eco-friendliness.

At the core of pellet grills' environmental benefits lies their use of natural hardwood pellets as the primary fuel source. Unlike traditional charcoal or gas grills, which rely on non-renewable resources such as coal or propane, pellet grills utilize hardwood pellets made from compressed sawdust and wood shavings, a byproduct of the lumber industry. By recycling these waste materials into a clean-burning fuel source, pellet grills help reduce the demand for fossil fuels and minimize the environmental impact associated with traditional cooking methods.

Moreover, the combustion process of hardwood pellets in pellet grills produces minimal emissions and ash compared to traditional charcoal or gas grills. This clean-burning nature reduces air pollution and promotes a healthier outdoor cooking environment by minimizing exposure to harmful chemicals and carcinogens.

Additionally, the design and operation of pellet grills contribute to their environmental sustainability. Pellet grills feature enclosed cooking chambers and insulated construction, which help contain heat and minimize heat loss during cooking. This energy-efficient design reduces fuel consumption and ensures consistent cooking temperatures, improving cooking efficiency and reducing environmental impact. Moreover, many pellet grills are equipped with advanced temperature control systems and built-in sensors that optimize fuel usage and cooking performance, enhancing their eco-friendliness.

Furthermore, the versatility and efficiency of pellet grills in outdoor cooking contribute to their environmental sustainability. With the ability to smoke, grill, roast, bake, and more, pellet grills offer a one-stop solution for all your outdoor culinary needs, reducing the need for multiple cooking appliances and minimizing energy consumption.

Moreover, using hardwood pellets in pellet grills promotes sustainable forestry practices and helps reduce waste in the lumber industry. By repurposing sawdust and wood shavings into a valuable fuel source, pellet grills support responsible forestry management and conservation efforts, ensuring that forests remain healthy and vibrant for future generations.

The Working Mechanism of a Pallet Grill

Pellet grills operate on a sophisticated mechanism designed to deliver precise temperature control and optimal cooking conditions while minimizing environmental impact. The complex process begins with the introduction of wood pellets into a designated storage container known as a hopper. These pellets serve as the grill's primary fuel source and are the foundation of its distinctive flavor profile.

Once the hopper is filled with wood pellets, the next step is for the pellets to be gradually fed into the cooking chamber by an auger, a spiral-shaped device powered by electricity. This controlled feeding mechanism ensures a consistent supply of pellets to sustain the cooking process without interruptions.

As the wood pellets enter the cooking chamber, they undergo combustion, igniting to produce the heat necessary for cooking. Unlike traditional grills that rely on charcoal or gas for fuel, pellet grills utilize the natural energy of wood pellets, eliminating the need for gasoline or open flames to ignite the fire.

Simultaneously, intake fans draw in air to regulate combustion and maintain optimal airflow within the cooking chamber. This airflow serves multiple purposes, including fueling the combustion of wood pellets, dispersing heat evenly throughout the cooking area, and circulating smoke to impart flavor to the food being prepared.

One of the distinguishing features of pellet grills is their ability to generate both heat and smoke simultaneously, creating an ideal cooking environment for a wide range of culinary applications. The combination of heat and smoke infuses meats, vegetables, and other ingredients with rich, smoky flavors that enhance their taste and aroma, elevating the overall dining experience.

Furthermore, the controlled combustion process in pellet grills allows for precise temperature regulation, allowing users to adjust the heat settings to suit their specific cooking needs.

Precise Temperature Control

One of the prominent features of pellet grills that sets them apart from traditional cooking methods is their precise temperature control capabilities. Pellet grills offer users the convenience of digital or dial-based temperature control, allowing for effortless adjustments to suit a variety of cooking techniques and preferences.

Moreover, pellet grills have advanced digital temperature control systems that give users unprecedented accuracy and convenience. These digital controllers feature intuitive interfaces that allow users to set their desired cooking temperature with a button, eliminating the guesswork and uncertainty associated with traditional cooking methods.

With digital temperature control, users can easily adjust the cooking temperature in increments of a few degrees, ensuring precise control over the cooking process. Whether you're slow-smoking a brisket for hours or searing a steak at high temperatures, the digital controller maintains consistent heat levels throughout the cooking process, resulting in evenly cooked and deliciously flavored dishes.

Furthermore, digital temperature control systems often come equipped with additional features such as built-in meat probes and programmable cooking presets, further enhancing the cooking experience. Meat probes allow users to monitor the internal temperature of their food in real time, ensuring that meats are cooked to the desired level of doneness without the risk of overcooking or undercooking. Programmable cooking presets enable users to save their favorite temperature settings for quick and easy access, streamlining the cooking process and saving time.

In addition to digital temperature control, many pellet grills also feature dial-based temperature control mechanisms for users who prefer a more traditional approach. These dial controls allow users to adjust the cooking temperature manually by turning a dial or knob, offering a tactile and intuitive interface for temperature adjustment.

With dial-based temperature control, users can fine-tune the cooking temperature to their specifications, whether they prefer slow and low cooking for tender and flavorful results or high-temperature grilling for a caramelized crust and juicy interior. Pellet grills' wide temperature range, typically 180°F to 500°F, allows for versatile cooking options to suit a variety of recipes and cooking styles.

Meat Probes

Meat probes, known as temperature probes or thermometers, are small, durable devices inserted into the meat during cooking to monitor its internal temperature. In pellet grills, these probes are often equipped with advanced sensors that connect to the grill's control board, allowing for seamless integration into the cooking process.

The primary function of meat probes in pellet grills is to provide users with accurate and reliable information about the internal temperature of their food. By monitoring the temperature of the meat throughout the cooking process, users can ensure that it reaches the desired level of doneness without the risk of overcooking or undercooking. This level of precision is particularly crucial when cooking large cuts of meat, such as brisket or pork shoulder, which require long cooking times and careful temperature management to achieve optimal results.

One key benefit of meat probes in pellet grills is their ability to connect directly to the grill's control board, allowing for automated temperature monitoring and adjustment. When the meat probe is inserted into the meat and connected to the control board, the grill's temperature control system can adjust the cooking temperature based on the desired internal temperature of the meat. This ensures that the meat is cooked to perfection without the user needing constant monitoring or manual temperature adjustments.

Moreover, meat probes allow users to customize their cooking experience according to their preferences and needs. Many pellet grills allow users to set custom temperature targets for different types of meat, allowing for precise control over the cooking process.

Additionally, meat probes provide valuable feedback to users about the progress of their cooking, allowing them to make informed decisions about when to remove the meat from the grill. By monitoring the internal temperature of the meat in real-time, users can avoid the common pitfalls of overcooking or undercooking and ensure that their dishes are served at the peak of perfection.

In short, meat probes play a vital role in enhancing precision cooking in pellet grills, allowing users to monitor their food's internal temperature with accuracy and reliability. By connecting to the grill's control board and providing real-time feedback about the progress of the cooking process, meat probes empower users to achieve optimal results every time, ensuring that their dishes are cooked to perfection and enjoyed to the fullest.

Chapter 4:

Cleaning

Maintaining a high standard of cleanliness is critical in any cooking activity, particularly when the methods involve direct heat and smoke, as with pellet grills. At the heart of any great culinary experience is the assurance of safety and cleanliness. Hygiene in the cooking process affects not only the taste and visual appeal of the food but also the health of those who consume the meal. When cooking surfaces and equipment are not adequately cleaned, they can nurture bacteria and residues that may contaminate food, potentially leading to foodborne illnesses. Moreover, the presence of old grease and food particles can influence the dishes' flavors, often negatively. Ensuring that the cooking equipment, especially pellet grills, is clean is therefore essential for both safety and quality.

Due to their unique cooking style and mechanisms, the importance of cleanliness becomes even more pronounced when dealing with pellet grills. Pellet grills, which burn wood pellets to generate smoke and heat, can accumulate ash, grease, and food residues in various parts of the grill over time. If not cleaned regularly, these residues can create a breeding ground for bacteria. They can also clog the mechanisms that deliver pellets and air, leading to inefficient operation and potentially hazardous conditions.

Proper cleaning and maintenance of pellet grills are vital to prevent such issues. Regular removal of ash ensures that the grill maintains adequate airflow, which is necessary for the safe and efficient combustion of the pellets. Similarly, cleaning the grates and interior surfaces of the grill helps remove carcinogenic substances that can form when meat is cooked at high temperatures. Regularly cleaning these surfaces reduces the risk of these substances contaminating your food and posing health risks.

In addition to safety and performance, cleanliness impacts the longevity of cooking equipment. Pellet grills, composed of numerous components, including electrical systems, motors, and augers, can suffer from the corrosive effects of ash and moisture if not regularly cleaned. The acidic nature of wood ash, combined with moisture from cooking and the environment, can lead to metal parts' corrosion and mechanical components' premature failure.

Regular cleaning and maintenance ensure that the grill operates at peak efficiency and prevents the deterioration of its parts, thereby extending the equipment's lifespan. This saves money in the long term and ensures that the grill remains a reliable tool in your culinary arsenal.

Lastly, a clean cooking environment enhances the overall culinary experience. Working with a clean and well-maintained pellet grill ensures that the focus remains on the creativity and enjoyment of cooking rather than on malfunctioning equipment or off-flavors caused by residue from previous cooking sessions.

Remember, every cook is responsible for maintaining cleanliness. This commitment extends beyond simple aesthetics; it is about safeguarding the health of those who enjoy the meals and preserving the integrity of the cooking process itself. Implementing routine cleaning protocols and adhering to hygiene standards becomes a foundational practice that enhances every aspect of the cooking experience.

How to Clean Your Pellet Grills?

Proper cleaning of your pellet grill is essential for maintaining its performance, extending its lifespan, and ensuring the safety and quality of your food. Following are some of the critical cleaning steps that will help you ensure the proper cleanliness of your pellet grills.

Take out the Removable Parts

Start by powering off your pellet grill and ensuring it is completely cool to the touch to avoid any risk of burns. Begin the cleaning process by disassembling the grill. Remove all removable parts, including the grates, grease tray, heat deflector, and any other components designed to be removed. This disassembly allows easier access to all grill areas, making cleaning more thorough.

Clean Removable Components Separately

Clean each removable component separately. Grates can be cleaned using a grill brush, steel wool, and soapy water. Soaking in hot water and dish soap for several hours can help loosen the residue for extremely grimy grates. Similarly, clean the grease tray and heat deflector, removing all grease and food residues. These components are crucial to clean thoroughly as they directly impact the flavor and safety of the cooked food.

Use the Vacuum Cleaner to Clean the Debris

Once the removable parts are set aside, use a shop vacuum or a handheld vacuum cleaner designed for outdoor use to remove ash and debris from the grill's interior. Pay special attention to the firepot, where pellets are burned, and most ash accumulates.

Regular removal of ash is crucial as it ensures that air can circulate properly, which is essential for the grill's efficient operation. Additionally, vacuum out the pellet hopper to remove dust and fragments that could affect the feed system.

Clean the Lid

The inside of the grill lid can accumulate a significant amount of smoke residue and grease over time. To clean the lid, use a grill cleaner or a mixture of warm water and mild dish soap with a sponge or cloth. Avoid abrasive tools or harsh chemicals that could damage the lid's finish. After scrubbing, rinse with clean water and wipe down with a dry cloth to prevent any streaks or water spots. This is the only way to maintain a clean and hygienic pellet grill.

Scrape the Edges, Chimney, and other Internal Parts Properly

With the significant debris and ash removed, focus on scrubbing the grill's edges, chimney, and other internal parts. For this task, a grill brush or a putty knife should be used to scrape off carbon build-up and stuck-on grease. Be thorough but gentle to avoid damaging any surfaces. For particularly tough residues, you can apply a degreaser, let it sit for a few minutes, and then scrub and wipe clean. Ensure all areas are washed well, including under the lid and around the seals, where grease and smoke can collect.

Vacuum Again to Remove Scraped Debris

Once you have scraped off the carbon build-up and other residues from the interior surfaces of your pellet grill, performing another round of vacuuming is essential. This step is critical to remove all loosened debris from the grill altogether. A thorough vacuum helps prevent any residual ash or debris from affecting the grill's performance or the flavor of the food during subsequent uses. Make sure to vacuum the firepot again and the areas around the hopper and beneath the cooking chamber where ash tends to accumulate.

Clean the Thermometer and Grease Chute

The accuracy of the grill thermometer is vital for effective cooking and maintaining desired temperatures. Begin by gently wiping the thermometer with a damp cloth. Avoid using abrasive materials or cleaners that could damage its surface or impair its function.

Similarly, the grease chute must be kept clean, which plays a critical role in managing grease runoff and preventing flare-ups. Use a narrow brush or a specialized cleaning tool to clear out grease accumulation within the chute. Ensuring these components are clean promotes safety and enhances the overall efficiency of your pellet grill.

Apply BBQ Cleaner to the Grill's Exterior

After thoroughly cleaning the internal components, it's essential to address the grill's exterior. Apply a high-quality BBQ cleaner suitable for your grill's finish. Spray or apply the cleaner as directed by the product instructions, covering all external surfaces, including the lid, side shelves, and legs. Use a microfiber cloth or a non-abrasive sponge to gently wipe the surfaces, removing dust, dirt, or grease spots. This helps maintain the grill's aesthetic appeal and provides a protective layer against weather elements and rust.

Protect through Polishing

Applying a polish after cleaning pellet grills with stainless steel or coated surfaces can help restore shine and provide additional protection against fingerprints and smudges. Ensure the polish is suitable for food-grade surfaces. Apply a small amount of polish using a soft cloth, working in circular motions until the surface is shiny and even. This step not only enhances the appearance of your grill but also contributes to its longevity and durability.

After-Cleaning Inspection

After cleaning and reassembling your pellet grill, inspect thoroughly to ensure everything is in proper order. Check all connections and fittings for tightness, especially around the hopper and auger mechanism. Inspect the seals around the lid and cooking chamber for any signs of wear or damage that could affect the grill's efficiency. This proactive approach helps identify potential issues that could lead to problems during cooking sessions.

Schedule Regular Cleaning

Regular cleaning should be an integral part of your pellet grill maintenance routine. Depending on your usage, a complete deep cleaning every few months is advisable, while a simpler clean, like wiping down surfaces and emptying the ash, should be done more frequently. A good practice is to perform a quick clean after every use, remove ash and wipe down grates, and do a deeper clean every few months, as described in these steps. Keeping a consistent cleaning schedule not only prolongs the life of your grill but also ensures that it remains safe, efficient, and ready to deliver excellent cooking results at any time.

Conclusion

Remember, each step in the cleaning process of your pellet grill is crucial for maintaining optimal performance and safety. Each step of the cleaning process is designed to ensure that your grill operates at its best, providing delicious results safely and efficiently. By thoroughly cleaning the grill's interior and exterior, ensuring all components are functioning correctly, and protecting the surfaces against environmental factors, you are investing in the longevity and reliability of your cooking appliance. This detailed attention to maintenance allows you to enjoy uninterrupted and satisfying barbecuing experiences with your pellet grill.

Chapter 5:

Beneficial Accessories

When diving into the world of pellet grilling, one quickly realizes that the grill itself is just the beginning. Investing in the right accessories is essential to maximize the capabilities of your pellet grill and elevate your cooking experience. Accessories enhance the functionality of your pellet grill and expand the variety of culinary techniques you can employ, from smoking and searing to baking and roasting.

Accessories for pellet grills are not merely additions; they are integral components that can significantly influence the efficiency, ease, and outcome of your cooking. They serve several purposes: protecting your equipment, improving its operational flexibility, and enriching the cooking experience by allowing for precision and variety beyond traditional grilling. Let's discuss some of the essential functions of pellet grill accessories to understand their impact on your cooking experience properly.

Enhance Grill's Functionality

The primary advantage of accessorizing your pellet grill is its enhanced functionality. Each accessory is designed to aid in specific aspects of the cooking process or to overcome certain limitations of a standard pellet grill. For instance, heat-resistant gloves and grill lights are essential for safety and convenience, allowing you to operate your grill in various weather conditions and at different times of the day. Similarly, using a grill cover protects your investment from the elements, which is crucial for maintaining your grill in optimal condition and extending its lifespan.

Expand Cooking Versatility

Pellet grill accessories open up a world of culinary possibilities. With the right tools, you can use your grill for more than barbecuing. A pizza stone, for instance, can transform your pellet grill into a pizza oven, allowing you to cook artisan pizzas right in your backyard. Similarly, a cast iron skillet will enable you to perfectly cook breakfast items like pancakes and eggs or even sear steaks and burgers. These accessories add versatility to your cooking reservoir and help achieve the perfect texture and flavor for various dishes.

Assist in Achieving Precision in Cooking

Accessories can also help you achieve greater precision in your cooking methods. Tools such as meat probes and digital thermometers are essential for monitoring temperatures accurately. These devices ensure you maintain the right cooking environment for your food, leading to consistently excellent results. They are particularly important when cooking temperature-sensitive items like briskets or ribs, where maintaining a specific temperature is critical for achieving perfect tenderness and flavor.

Increase Convenience and Efficiency

Some accessories are designed to increase the convenience and efficiency of using your pellet grill. Pellet storage containers, for example, keep your wood pellets dry and ready to use, ensuring optimal grill performance. Ash vacuums and cleaning kits simplify the cleanup process, making it easier to maintain your grill after each use. These conveniences ensure that your grilling experience is as enjoyable and hassle-free as possible, allowing you more time to focus on what truly matters: cooking and enjoying good food with family and friends.

Enhance Flavor and Aesthetic

Beyond functionality and convenience, certain accessories can enhance your meals' flavor and aesthetic appeal. Smoker boxes, for example, allow for the introduction of various wood flavors, letting you infuse your food with subtle hints of hickory, cherry, or mesquite, depending on your preferences. This enhances the taste and adds an element of gourmet cooking to your grilling sessions. Additionally, specialized tools like rib racks and chicken throne beer can holders optimize space and improve cooking efficiency, ensuring even cooking and perfect presentation.

Personalize Your Grilling Experience

Lastly, pellet grill accessories allow you to personalize your grilling experience to suit your specific culinary preferences and needs. The right accessories can cater to every requirement, making every grilling session uniquely yours.

Essential Accessories for a Pellet Grill

The accessories utilized extensively influence the enhancement and optimization of the cooking process in pellet grilling. Let us discuss some fundamental accessories that every pellet grill owner should consider essential. Each of the following accessories ensures the grilling experience is efficient, precise, and enjoyable.

Wood Pellets

Wood pellets are the first and perhaps most crucial accessory for any pellet grill. Pellet grills are unique because they use specially designed pellets made from compressed wood as fuel, providing both heat and smoke for cooking and flavoring the food. The choice of pellets can significantly affect the taste and efficiency of the grilling process.

Different types of wood pellets offer varying flavors and are suitable for various kinds of meats and dishes. For instance, hickory pellets provide a strong, smoky flavor perfect for robust meats like beef and pork, while applewood imparts a sweeter, milder smoke ideal for poultry and fish. Moreover, high-quality, low-moisture pellets are crucial as they burn cleaner and more efficiently, producing less ash and more consistent heat.

Thermometer

A reliable thermometer is another indispensable tool for any pellet grill user. Cooking meats to perfection requires precise temperature control, and while many pellet grills come equipped with built-in thermometers, an additional digital meat thermometer can provide more accuracy. These devices allow you to monitor the internal temperature of your food without opening the grill, thus maintaining a consistent cooking environment.

Digital thermometers often feature probes that can be inserted into the meat and readouts that provide instant temperature readings. Some advanced models can connect to smartphones through Bluetooth or Wi-Fi, allowing chefs to keep an eye on their food from a distance, ensuring that every meal is cooked to precise specifications without constant manual checking.

Brushes

Maintaining a clean grill is essential for the appliance's longevity and the safety and quality of the food prepared on it. Brushes are a fundamental tool for keeping your pellet grill in prime condition. A good grill brush should have robust bristles that can effectively remove food residue, grease, and ash from the grill grates without damaging them.

Several types of brushes are available, including those with stainless steel, brass, or nylon bristles. Each type has its advantages and specific uses. Stainless steel brushes are durable and practical at scraping off harsh residues but should be used cautiously on porcelain-coated grates to avoid scratching. Brass bristles are softer and safer for such surfaces but may not last as long. Nylon brushes, however, are best used for cold cleaning and are gentle on all types of surfaces.

Tool Set

A high-quality tool set is vital for any pellet grill owner. This set typically includes tongs, a spatula, and sometimes a fork or basting brush, all designed to handle the rigors of grilling. Tongs are essential for turning and positioning food precisely without piercing it, which helps retain juices and flavors. A spatula with a wide surface is ideal for safely flipping burgers, fish, and other delicate items that might break apart.

These tools are usually made of stainless steel for durability and longevity, featuring long handles to keep hands away from the heat. Some sets might also include silicone basting brushes, which are excellent for directly putting marinades and sauces on food on the grill. Investing in a toolset specifically designed for grilling can significantly enhance the ease and safety of managing food on a hot grill.

Covers

Protective covers are another essential accessory for any pellet grill. A cover protects the grill from the external elements, ensuring it remains clean and dry when unused. This is particularly important in preventing rust and wear from moisture, dust, and sunlight exposure.

Quality covers are usually made from heavy-duty materials like polyester or vinyl that are waterproof and UV-resistant. A good cover fits easily over the grill, often with ties or Velcro straps to secure it against wind and weather. Maintaining a grill with a proper cover can extend the life of the pellet grill significantly, safeguarding the investment made into high-quality outdoor cooking equipment.

Marinades and Rubs

Marinades and rubs enhance the flavor of the food cooked on a pellet grill. Marinades typically consist of acidic ingredients like vinegar or citrus juice mixed with oils and spices, which help to tenderize and infuse the meat with flavor. On the other hand, rubs are dry mixes of spices and herbs that are applied directly to the surface of the meat before cooking.

Both marinades and rubs can be customized according to the type of meat and the desired flavor profile. For instance, a vigorous rub with coffee and chili powder works well with beef, while a citrusy marinade can elevate the delicate flavors of fish or poultry. The slow-cooking process of pellet grills allows the flavors from marinades and rubs to penetrate the meat deeply, creating complex flavor profiles that are difficult to achieve with quicker cooking methods.

Conclusion

The addition of well-chosen accessories can significantly enhance the pellet grilling experience. These accessories not only aid in the practical aspects of grilling but also in protecting your equipment and elevating the flavors of your food. Each plays a unique role in the process, from preparation to preservation, ensuring that every pellet grilling session is as rewarding and enjoyable as possible. With these essential accessories, outdoor cooking lovers can expect superior performance and longevity from their pellet grills, making every barbecue memorable.

Chapter 6:

Rubs

The Importance of Rubs for Flavorful BBQ

Few elements are as integral to flavor development as rubs in any barbecue experience. These blends of herbs, spices, salts, and sugars are not only a feature of barbecue tradition but also serve as the foundation upon which the entire flavor profile of a dish is built. Here is why rubs are important for a flavorful BBQ experience.

Enhance Flavors

Rubs are vital in enhancing the flavor profiles of meats, poultry, seafood, and even vegetables. By carefully selecting and blending various ingredients, barbecue enthusiasts can create rubs that impart complex layers of flavor to their dishes. Combining aromatic spices like paprika, cumin, and garlic with sweeteners like brown sugar or honey establishes a balance of savory, sweet, and spicy notes that tantalize the taste buds.

Tenderizing and Moisturizing

Beyond flavor enhancement, rubs serve practical purposes in barbecue cooking. Many rub ingredients, such as salt, sugar, and acidic components like citrus zest or vinegar, act as natural tenderizers and moisturizers for meats. When applied to the surface of the meat, these ingredients penetrate the muscle fibers, helping to break down tough tissues and retain moisture during the cooking process. As a result, the meat becomes more tender, succulent, and flavorful, making for a more enjoyable eating experience.

Creates a Crust

Another essential function of rubs is the creation of a flavorful crust on the meat's exterior. As the meat cooks, the sugars and spices in the rub caramelize and form a savory crust that adds texture and depth of flavor. This crust not only enhances the appearance of the meat but also locks in juices, resulting in a moist and flavorful interior.

Customization and Creativity

Rubs' most significant advantages are their versatility and the opportunity they offer for customization and creativity. Barbecue enthusiasts can tailor their rubs to suit their personal taste preferences and the specific characteristics of the meat being cooked. Whether it's adjusting the spice level, experimenting with different herbs and spices, or incorporating unique ingredients like coffee grounds or cocoa powder, the possibilities for creating unique flavor profiles are endless.

In short, rubs are an essential component of flavorful barbecue cooking, offering various benefits, including flavor enhancement, tenderization, moisture retention, and creating a savory crust. By carefully selecting and crafting rub blends to complement the characteristics of the meat, barbecue enthusiasts can elevate their dishes to new heights of taste and texture. With creativity, experimentation, and attention to detail, rubs can transform ordinary barbecue into extraordinary culinary delights, ensuring every bite is a truly memorable experience.

Application Techniques

Applying rubs effectively is as important as selecting the right blend of ingredients. To ensure even distribution and maximum flavor penetration, it is recommended to generously coat the meat with the rub, pressing it firmly into the surface to adhere. For more significant cuts of meat, such as brisket or pork shoulder, it is beneficial to apply the rub for several hours or even overnight before cooking, allowing the flavors to permeate the meat thoroughly. Applying the rub just before cooking for more minor cuts or quicker cooking times can yield delicious results.

How Rubs Can Impact the Flavor of the Meat?

Rubs are the central component of barbecue and grilling, serving as a flavorful foundation that can transform ordinary meats into culinary masterpieces. Rubs are applied to meats before cooking to enhance their flavor, texture, and overall appeal by combining herbs, spices, salts, sugars, and sometimes additional ingredients. The impact of rubs on meat flavor is significant, influencing every aspect of the cooking process and ultimately delivering a sensational dining experience. Let's discuss the effects of rubs on meat flavor.

Flavor Infusion

The primary function of a rub is to infuse meats with various flavors. Each component contributes to a complex and harmonious flavor profile. When applied to the surface of the meat, these ingredients penetrate the outer layers, imparting their essence throughout the cooking process.

The heat activates the spices and herbs as the meat cooks, releasing their essential oils and aromatic compounds. This process flavors the meat's exterior and infuses the interior as the seasonings penetrate deeper into the muscle fibers. The result is a depth of flavor that evolves and intensifies with each bite, ensuring that every mouthful is a delicious sensation of spices, herbs, and savory goodness.

Balancing Sweet, Savory, and Spicy Notes

A well-balanced rub combines sweet, savory, and spicy notes, creating a delightful contrast of flavors that excites the palate. The combination of sugars like brown sugar or honey with savory elements like salt and garlic forms the backbone of many rubs, providing a harmonious blend that complements the meat's natural flavors.

Adding spices such as paprika, chili powder, black pepper, or cayenne pepper adds complexity and depth. These spices contribute heat and spiciness and enhance flavor, ensuring a well-rounded and satisfying taste experience. The careful selection and proportion of ingredients in a rub are crucial to achieving the perfect balance of flavors that enhance rather than overpower the meat.

Adding Depth and Complexity

Rubs add depth and complexity to meats, elevating them from ordinary to extraordinary. Combining multiple spices and herbs creates a diverse flavor profile that unfolds with each bite. For example, a rub containing smoked paprika, cumin, and coriander can impart a rich, earthy flavor with a subtle smokiness. At the same time, a blend of garlic, onion, and herbs like thyme and rosemary adds freshness and herbaceous notes.

The cooking process further enhances the depth of flavor achieved through rubs. As the meat cooks low and slow over a barbecue or grill, the flavors intensify and meld together, creating a cohesive and satisfying taste sensation. The result is a dish that satisfies the taste buds and engages the senses with its complexity and depth.

Why You Should Not Rub Them into the Meat

Contrary to the term "rub," it is not advisable to vigorously massage or rub the seasoning mixture into the meat. Doing so can adversely affect the final outcome of the dish. Rubbing the seasoning too aggressively can cause the spices to become compacted, resulting in uneven distribution and potentially overpowering pockets of flavor in some areas while leaving others bland. Moreover, excessive rubbing can damage the surface of the meat, disrupting the natural juices and texture and leading to a less desirable eating experience.

Instead of rubbing the seasoning into the meat, a gentle patting motion is recommended to ensure the rub adheres evenly to the surface without compacting the spices or causing damage. This gentle application technique allows for optimal flavor penetration while preserving the integrity of the meat. Additionally, allowing the seasoned meat to rest before cooking allows the flavors to meld and develop, resulting in a more harmonious and well-rounded flavor profile.

RECIPES

Maple Baby Back Ribs

Ingredients:

* 2 racks of baby back ribs

* 1 cup maple syrup

* ½ cup soy sauce

* ¼ cup apple cider vinegar

* 2 cloves garlic, minced

* 1 teaspoon smoked paprika

* 1 teaspoon black pepper

* ½ teaspoon salt

* 2 tablespoons olive oil

Instructions:

1. For better marinade absorption, strip the thin membrane from the underside of the ribs.
2. In a mixing bowl, blend together the maple syrup, soy sauce, apple cider vinegar, minced garlic, black pepper, smoked paprika, salt, and olive oil until well mixed.
3. Place the ribs in either a spacious baking dish or a resealable plastic bag. Pour the marinade all over, ensuring it covers every bit. If utilizing the plastic bag, maintain its seal and gently massage the marinade into the ribs. Let the ribs marinate in the refrigerator for at least 4 hours, preferably overnight.

4. After marinating, take the ribs out of the refrigerator and let them come to room temperature for about 30 minutes.

5. Arrange the ribs on a baking sheet, ensuring the meaty side is facing up, and the sheet is directly lined with aluminum foil or parchment paper. Set aside the marinade for basting purposes.

6. Now, set the temperature on your pellet grill to 300°F (150°C).

7. Smoke the ribs on the pellet grill at 300°F (150°C). Remember to give them a good basting with the reserved marinade every 30 minutes to keep them moist and full of flavor. Cook the ribs well until they hit the internal temperature of 190-205°F (88-96°C) for tender, fall-off-the-bone perfection, which typically takes about 3-4 hours.

8. Once the ribs are cooked, carefully take them off the grill and let them rest for a few minutes before slicing and serving.

9. Serve the maple baby back ribs hot and toss some chopped fresh herbs like parsley or green onions if desired. Enjoy your delicious, sticky-sweet ribs!

Simple Smoked Baby Back Ribs

Ingredients:

* Baby back ribs (2 racks)

* Dry rub seasoning:

* 2 tablespoons brown sugar

* 1 tablespoon smoked paprika

* 1 tablespoon garlic powder

* 1 tablespoon onion powder

* 1 teaspoon black pepper

* 1 teaspoon salt

* Mix in 1 teaspoon of cayenne pepper (This ingredient is optional: for a bit of seasoning)

* BBQ sauce (optional for serving)

Instructions:

1. Start by preparing your pellet grill. Ensure you have enough pellets loaded in the hopper to maintain a consistent temperature of around 225°F (107°C) throughout the smoking process.

2. While you're at it, take a moment to remove the membrane from the back of the ribs. Simply slide a knife underneath, then grab hold of it with a paper towel for better grip and peel it off.

3. In a small bowl, combine all the dry rub seasoning ingredients until they're thoroughly mixed. Then, take your ribs and pat them dry with some paper towels. Once they're dry, generously season both sides of the racks with

the dry rub, really getting in there and massaging it into the meat to make sure it's fully coated.

4. Once your pellet grill hits that sweet spot temperature, lay those seasoned ribs on the grill grate, bone side down. Shut the lid and let them soak up that smoky goodness for roughly 3 hours, making sure to keep the temperature steady between 225°F to 250°F (107°C to 121°C). If you're jazzing things up with wood chips for extra flavor, toss them in following the manufacturer's instructions.

5. After three hours of smoking, it's time to check on those ribs. They should have a nice bark on the outside, and the meat should be pulled back from the bones. To test for doneness, try poking a toothpick between the bones—it should slip in effortlessly, showing they're tender and ready.

6. If desired, you can glaze the ribs with the BBQ sauce during the final 30 minutes of cooking. Just brush it onto both sides of the ribs and let it cook until it caramelizes on the surface.

7. Once the ribs are finished, take them off the grill and give them a rest for roughly 10 minutes before you start slicing. This way, all those tasty juices get a chance to spread out through the meat, making it extra flavorful and tender.

8. Cut those racks between the bones and dish up those mouthwatering smoked baby back ribs piping hot, accompanied by your favorite sides and extra BBQ sauce for dipping. Enjoy the tender, flavorful goodness with friends and family!

Smoked Spare Ribs

Ingredients:

* Spare ribs (2 racks)
* Dry rub seasoning:
* 3 tablespoons brown sugar
* 2 tablespoons smoked paprika
* 1 tablespoon garlic powder
* 1 tablespoon onion powder
* 1 tablespoon ground mustard
* 1 tablespoon chili powder
* 1 tablespoon salt
* 1 teaspoon black pepper
* BBQ sauce (optional, for serving)

Instructions:

1. Prepare your pellet grill and bring the temperature to 225°F (107°C). Before placing the spare ribs on the grill, make sure you remove the membrane from the back and trim off any excess fat according to your preference.
2. In a bowl, combine all the ingredients for the dry rub seasoning. Apply a generous amount to both sides of the spare ribs, making sure it's evenly distributed.
3. Position the seasoned spare ribs on the pellet grill, bone side facing down. Close the lid and smoke for around 5-6 hours, keeping the temperature persistent at 225°F (107°C). Feel free to introduce wood chips or chunks for extra smoky flavor.

4. Check the ribs after 5-6 hours to gauge their tenderness. Look for a delightful bark and meat that's tender, readily pulling apart with a gentle tug.
5. If desired, you can opt to coat the ribs with BBQ sauce during the final hour of smoking to impart a sweet and tangy glaze.
6. Once the ribs are finished, take them off the grill and allow them to rest for approximately 10-15 minutes. This crucial step allows the juices to spread within the meat, ensuring maximum flavor and tenderness.
7. Slice the spare ribs between the bones and serve hot, accompanied by your favorite sides and extra BBQ sauce if desired. Enjoy the smoky, tender goodness of these delicious smoked spare ribs!

Classic Pulled Pork

Ingredients:

* Pork shoulder or pork butt (6-8 pounds)
* Dry rub seasoning:
* 1/4 cup brown sugar
* 2 tablespoons smoked paprika
* 1 tablespoon garlic powder
* 1 tablespoon onion powder
* 1 tablespoon salt
* 1 tablespoon black pepper
* Mix in 1 teaspoon of cayenne pepper (This ingredient is optional: for a bit of seasoning)
* Apple cider vinegar (for spritzing)
* BBQ sauce (optional, for serving)
* Hamburger buns or sandwich rolls (for serving)

Instructions:

1. Begin by preparing your pellet grill for low and slow cooking. Preheat it to 225°F (107°C).
2. If desired, trim off any extra fat from the pork shoulder. However, you can leave some fat to maintain moisture during smoking. Carefully dab the pork with paper towels until it's thoroughly dried.
3. In a bowl, combine all the ingredients for the dry rub seasoning. Then, generously coat the pork shoulder with the mixture, ensuring that it's rubbed evenly over all sides.

4. Position the seasoned pork shoulder directly on the pellet grill, ensuring the fat side is facing up. Close the lid and allow it to smoke for several hours until reaching an internal temperature of approximately 195°F to 205°F (90°C to 96°C). Expect this slow-cooking process to span anywhere from 10 to 14 hours, varying based on the pork shoulder's size and temperature consistency.

5. At intervals of approximately one hour, spritz the pork shoulder with apple cider vinegar to maintain moisture and enrich the flavor. This practice also helps to develop a beautiful bark on the exterior of the meat.

6. Once the pork shoulder reaches the desired internal temperature and is tender enough to easily shred with a fork, it's ready to be removed from the pellet grill.

7. Move the smoked pork shoulder to a cutting board or wrap it in aluminum foil, allowing it to rest for at least 30 minutes.

8. With either two forks or meat claws, shred the smoked pork shoulder into bite-sized pieces. Remove any sizable pieces of fat or connective tissue as needed.

9. Set forth the pulled pork on hamburger buns or sandwich rolls, with a side of your favorite BBQ sauce for those desiring an intensified flavor experience.

10. Enjoy the tender, smoky goodness of this classic pulled pork, perfect for sandwiches, tacos, or even on its own!

Apple-Smoked Pulled Pork

Ingredients:

* **Pork Shoulder (6-8 pounds)**

* **Dry Rub Seasoning:**

* 1/4 cup brown sugar

* 2 tablespoons smoked paprika

* 1 tablespoon garlic powder

* 1 tablespoon onion powder

* 1 tablespoon salt

* 1 tablespoon black pepper

* 1 teaspoon ground cinnamon

* **Applewood Chunks or Chips** (for smoking)

* **Spritzing Liquid:**

* Apple juice or apple cider vinegar

* **Optional:**

* BBQ sauce (for serving)

* Hamburger buns or sandwich rolls (for serving)

Instructions:

1. Adjust your pellet grill to 225°F (107°C) and let it heat up. Toss in some applewood chunks or chips to give the smoke a nice apple flavor.
2. Trim the pork shoulder, taking off the extra fat but leaving a thin layer to keep it moist during smoking. Blot it dry with paper towels to ensure it's nice and dry.

3. Then, whisk together brown sugar, smoked paprika, onion powder, garlic powder, salt, black pepper, and ground cinnamon in a bowl for the dry rub.

4. Spread the seasoning mixture all over the pork shoulder, ensuring it's well-covered from top to bottom.

5. Set the seasoned pork shoulder on the pellet grill, making sure the fat side is facing upwards. Then, close the lid and maintain a constant temperature of 225°F (107°C) throughout the smoking process.

6. Spritz the pork shoulder with apple juice or apple cider vinegar on an hourly basis to keep it fully moist and amplify the apple essence. This trick also contributes to forming a flavorful bark.

7. Smoke the pork for approximately 10-12 hours until it reaches the desired tenderness. Use your handy meat thermometer to make sure it's hitting between 195°F to 205°F (90°C to 96°C). At this point, the meat should be tender enough to effortlessly shred with a fork.

8. Take the pork shoulder out of the grill with care and allow it to rest on a cutting board, or wrap it snugly in aluminum foil for at least half an hour.

9. It's shred o'clock! Use your forks or meat claws and shred the pork shoulder into bite-sized pieces. Don't forget to toss out any unwanted fat or chewy parts.

10. Sandwich or hamburger buns are perfect for serving the pulled pork, along with BBQ sauce on the side if desired. Enjoy the deliciously sweet and smoky applewood flavor in every bite!

Apple-Smoked Bacon

Ingredients:

* **Pork Belly (2-3 pounds)**

* **Dry Cure:**

* 1/4 cup kosher salt

* 2 tablespoons brown sugar

* 1 tablespoon black pepper

* 1 teaspoon garlic powder

* 1 teaspoon onion powder

* 1/2 teaspoon pink curing salt (optional for color and preservation)

* **Wood Chips:**

* Applewood chips (for smoking)

Instructions:

1. Grab that pork belly, rinse it well under cold water, and then pat it dry with some paper towels. Place it on a clean cutting board.

2. Now, use a small bowl and toss in some brown sugar, kosher salt, black pepper, garlic powder, onion powder, and pink curing salt (if using). Mix all those ingredients up until they are nicely combined.

3. Next, get hands-on and rub that dry mixture carefully all over the pork belly, ensuring that it is evenly coated on all sides. Once it's all coated up, transfer that pork belly into a big resealable bag or a container that seals up tight.

4. Seal it up, and into the fridge, it goes! Let the pork belly cure for 7-10 days, flipping it over every other day to ensure even curing.
5. Before smoking, soak applewood chips in water for at least 30 minutes. Prepare your pellet grill for indirect smoking at a temperature of 200-225°F (93-107°C).
6. Remove the cured pork belly from the refrigerator and rinse off the excess cure mixture under cold water. Pat it dry with some paper towels.
7. Put the pork belly on the grill, making sure there is space between each piece in order for smoke to circulate.
8. Add the soaked applewood chips to the pellet grill.
9. Let that bacon soak up the smoky goodness for a good 2-3 hours, or until it hits around 150-155°F (about 65-68°C).
10. Once it's done, just gently take it out and let it chill to room temperature.
11. If desired, stick the bacon in the fridge for smoother slicing. Grab a sharp knife or a meat slicer and slice it up to your desired thickness.
12. Cook the apple-smoked bacon in a skillet over medium heat until crispy and golden brown.
13. Plate up that crispy bacon next to your go-to breakfast staples, lay it in sandwiches for a satisfying crunch, or toss it into salads and soups for some flavorful twist. Enjoy the rich, smoky flavor of homemade applewood-smoked bacon!

Smoked Ham

Ingredients:

*   1 bone-in or boneless ham, preferably fully cooked (around 8-10 pounds)
*   1 cup brown sugar
*   1/2 cup honey
*   1/4 cup Dijon mustard
*   1/4 cup apple cider vinegar
*   2 tablespoons Worcestershire sauce
*   1 tablespoon smoked paprika
*   1 teaspoon garlic powder
*   1 teaspoon onion powder
*   1/2 teaspoon of black pepper
*   1/4 teaspoon cloves (optional, for extra depth)

Instructions:

1. Adjust your pellet grill to around 225°F (107°C). Aim for a consistent, ongoing temperature throughout the smoking process.
2. Grab a sharp knife and make criss-cross cuts on the ham's surface, forming diamond shapes and patterns. This helps the glaze soak in and create a lovely presentation.
3. Place the ham on the pellet grill and cut the side down if it's bone-in. Close the lid properly and let the ham smoke for approximately 3-4 hours.

4. Toss some applewood or hickory chips on the grill to give the ham that rich, smoky flavor. Applewood or hickory chips work well with ham.
5. Then, in a saucepan on medium heat, mix up brown sugar, honey, Dijon mustard, apple cider vinegar, Worcestershire sauce, smoked paprika, garlic powder, onion powder, black pepper, and cloves (if using).
6. Keep stirring that mix until the sugar's all melted and everything's blended nicely. Allow the glaze to simmer for 5-10 minutes or until it has slightly thickened.
7. After the ham has been smoked for about 2 hours, begin brushing the glaze over the surface of the ham every 30 minutes. Ensure the entire surface is coated evenly with the glaze.
8. Once the ham's internal temperature registers at 140°F (60°C), it's perfectly cooked. Just poke a meat thermometer into the ham's chunkiest section, making sure to avoid the bone.
9. If your ham's still pink in the middle, cook it until it's 160°F (71°C) before serving.
10. Once the ham is done, take it off from the grill and let it sit for 10-15 minutes before slicing.
11. Slice the smoked ham and serve it warm, drizzling any remaining glaze over the slices for an extra burst of flavor. Enjoy!

Smoked Pork Tenderloins

Ingredients:

* 2 pork tenderloins (about 1 pound each)

* 1/4 cup maple syrup

* 2 tablespoons soy sauce

* 2 tablespoons Dijon mustard

* 1 tablespoon apple cider vinegar

* 1 tablespoon olive oil

* 2 cloves garlic, minced

* 1 teaspoon smoked paprika

* 1/2 teaspoon black pepper

* 1/2 teaspoon salt

Instructions:

1. Blend soy sauce, maple syrup, Dijon mustard, olive oil, apple cider vinegar, minced garlic, black pepper, smoked paprika, and salt to create the marinade.

2. Lay the pork tenderloins carefully in a shallow dish or pop them into a resealable plastic bag, then cover them with the marinade, making sure they're fully coated. Marinate in the fridge for at least an hour or, for the best results, overnight.

3. Get your pellet grill up to 225°F (107°C) and use your chosen smoking wood chips or chunks, aiming for a stable temperature. Take the pork tenderloins out of the marinade and get rid of any extra marinade.

4. Place the pork tenderloins directly on the grill, leaving some space between them for the smoke to circulate.

5. Close the lid of the grill and let those tenderloins smoke for about 1 to 1.5 hours, or until they hit 145°F (63°C) inside. Just poke them carefully with a meat thermometer in the thickest part to check.

6. In a little saucepan, pour in the leftover marinade and get it bubbling over medium heat. Then, turn the heat down and let it simmer for 5-7 minutes until it thickens up a bit.

7. Brush the glaze over the smoked pork tenderloins during the last 15-20 minutes of smoking, ensuring they are evenly coated.

8. Once the pork tenderloins hit that perfect internal temperature and are all glossy with glaze, take them out of the grill and let them chill for 5-10 minutes before you slice into them.

9. Slice the smoked pork tenderloins into medallions and serve warm, drizzling any remaining glaze over the slices for extra flavor. Enjoy!

Tender Grilled Loin Chops

Ingredients:

* 4 loin chops (about 1 inch thick)

* Salt and pepper to taste

* 2 tablespoons olive oil

* 2 cloves garlic, minced

* 1 teaspoon dried thyme

* 1 teaspoon dried rosemary

* 1 teaspoon dried oregano

* 1/2 teaspoon paprika

* 1/4 teaspoon red pepper flakes (optional)

* 4 tablespoons unsalted butter, softened

* 2 tablespoons chopped fresh parsley

* 1 tablespoon chopped fresh chives

* 1 tablespoon lemon juice

* Lemon wedges for serving

Instructions:

1. Give those loin chops a good pat-down with some paper towels to get 'em nice and dry. Then, sprinkle on some salt and pepper on both sides.
2. Get that grill heated up to a solid medium-high heat, somewhere between 375-400°F (190-204°C).
3. Mix up some olive oil, minced garlic, dried rosemary, dried thyme, dried oregano, paprika, and red pepper

flakes (if you're feeling spicy). Rub that all over your chops and let them marinate for at least 15-20 minutes at room temperature.

4. Once the grill is hot, place the loin chops on the grill grate. Close the lid and sizzle for about 4-5 minutes on each side, or until they hit 145°F (63°C) for medium-rare or 160°F (71°C) for medium. Ensure accuracy by inserting the meat thermometer into the thickest portion.

5. While those chops are grilling away, mix together some softened butter, chives, fresh parsley, and lemon juice.

6. Once the loin chops are done grilling, transfer them to a serving platter.

7. Top each chop with a generous dollop of herb butter while they are still hot, allowing it to melt and infuse the chops with flavor.

8. Serve the grilled loin chops immediately with lemon wedges on the side for squeezing over the meat. Enjoy the juicy and flavorful grilled loin chops with your favorite sides!

Smoked Brisket

Ingredients:

* 1 whole beef brisket (10-12 pounds), untrimmed
* 1/4 cup kosher salt
* 1/4 cup black pepper, freshly ground
* 2 tablespoons smoked paprika
* 2 tablespoons garlic powder
* 2 tablespoons onion powder
* 2 tablespoons brown sugar
* 1 tablespoon ground mustard
* 1 tablespoon chili powder
* 1 tablespoon cumin
* 1 tablespoon coriander
* 1 tablespoon dried oregano
* 1 tablespoon dried thyme
* 1/2 cup using beef broth or water (for spritzing)
* Wood chunks or chips (preferably oak or mesquite)

Instructions:

1. Trim away any extra fat, but leave about a quarter-inch layer on the surface. That fat helps keep the meat juicy while it's smoking. Also, if you spot any tough stuff like silver skin or connective tissue, give it the boot. We want the meat to be as tender as possible when it's done!

2. Grab a bowl and toss in some kosher salt, black pepper, smoked paprika, garlic powder, onion powder, brown sugar, ground mustard, chili powder, cumin, coriander, dried oregano, and dried thyme to create the rub.
3. Get your grill preheated to 225°F (107°C), using your choice of wood chunks or chips.
4. Now, let's get hands-on with that brisket! Take your spice mixture and rub it all nicely over the brisket, making sure to cover every inch of it. Give it a good, gentle press to help the rub stick to the meat.
5. Gently place the brisket, fat-side up, onto the pellet grill. Close the lid and let it smoke for several hours, maintaining the temperature at 225°F (107°C).
6. After the first 3-4 hours of smoking, start spritzing the brisket with beef broth or water every hour to keep it moist and enhance the bark formation.
7. Smoke that brisket till it hits 195-205°F (90-96°C) internally. Poke it with the thermometer and give it time; it could be a good 10 to 14 hours, depending on how big and chunky it is.
8. Once the brisket is smoky perfection, remove it and wrap it tightly in either aluminum foil or a butcher paper. Let it rest in a cooler or insulated container for at least one hour.
9. Carefully unwrap it and then, using a sharp knife, slice against the grain into thin, juicy pieces. Ready to savor!

Burnt Ends

Ingredients:

For the Burnt Ends:

* 3-4 pounds of beef brisket point (also known as the deckle)
* 2 tablespoons kosher salt
* 2 tablespoons black pepper, freshly ground
* 2 tablespoons brown sugar
* 1 tablespoon smoked paprika
* 1 tablespoon garlic powder
* 1 tablespoon onion powder

For the Glaze:

* 1/2 cup ketchup
* 1/4 cup apple cider vinegar
* 1/4 cup honey or maple syrup
* 2 tablespoons Worcestershire sauce
* 1 tablespoon Dijon mustard
* 1 teaspoon smoked paprika
* 1/2 teaspoon garlic powder
* Salt and pepper to taste

Instructions:

1. Preheat it to a gentle 225°F (107°C), infusing your preferred wood chips or chunks for that signature smoky essence.

2. As the grill warms up, trim any surplus fat from the brisket point, ensuring just enough remains to lock in succulent juiciness throughout the smoking process. Slice the brisket point into cubes that are around 1 to 1.5 inches.

3. In a bowl, combine kosher salt, black pepper, brown sugar, smoked paprika, garlic powder, and onion powder to create the rub for the burnt ends.

4. Sprinkle that rub all over those brisket cubes, making sure they're covered on every side.

5. Place the seasoned brisket cubes on the pellet grill, leaving some space between each cube for the smoke to circulate.

6. Close the lid and let the burnt ends smoke for approximately 3-4 hours or until they develop a dark, caramelized crust (bark) on the outside.

7. Combine ketchup, apple cider vinegar, honey or maple syrup, Worcestershire sauce, Dijon mustard, smoked paprika, and garlic powder in a small saucepan—sprinkle with salt and pepper to taste.

8. Heat it up on medium, giving it a stir now and then until it thickens up a bit—merging all those flavors together. Remove from heat and set aside.

9. Once the burnt ends have been smoked for several hours and a caramelized crust has developed, transfer them to a large bowl. Pour the prepared glaze over the burnt ends and toss them gently to coat evenly.

10. Place the glazed burnt ends back on the pellet grill and let them smoke for an additional 30-60 minutes, allowing the glaze to caramelize and create a sticky, flavorful coating.
11. Once they're good to go, grab those delicious burnt ends from the grill and dish them out while they're still steaming. Enjoy!

Pulled Beef

Ingredients:

* 4-5 pounds beef chuck roast

* 1/4 cup olive oil

* 1/4 cup apple cider vinegar

* 2 tablespoons Worcestershire sauce

* 2 tablespoons soy sauce

* 1/4 cup brown sugar

* 2 tablespoons smoked paprika

* 1 tablespoon garlic powder

* 1 tablespoon onion powder

* 1 tablespoon chili powder

* 1 tablespoon kosher salt

* 1 teaspoon black pepper

* 1 teaspoon cumin

* 1 teaspoon dried thyme

* Wood chunks or chips (hickory or oak recommended)

Instructions:

1. In a big bowl, whisk together some olive oil, apple cider vinegar, Worcestershire sauce, soy sauce, and brown sugar.
2. Add smoked paprika, garlic powder, onion powder, chili powder, kosher salt, black pepper, cumin, and dried thyme to create the marinade.

3. Put the beef chuck roast in a big zip-top plastic bag or a shallow dish, and pour that marinade all over it. Make sure the roast gets a good coating. Stick it in the fridge and let it hang out for at least 4 hours, or even better, overnight.

4. Adjust your pellet grill to 225°F (107°C) using your preferred wood chunks or chips (hickory or oak works well for beef).

5. Remove the beef chuck roast from the marinade and let any excess marinade drip off.

6. Lay that roast on the pellet grill and let it smoke away for around 6 to 8 hours, or until the inside hits between 195 to 205°F (about 90 to 96°C) and the meat is tender enough to pull apart easily with a fork.

7. Don't forget to give that beef a spritz every hour with a mix of apple cider vinegar and water to keep it nice and juicy while also amping up that smoky flavor.

8. When the beef hits that sweet spot of internal temperature, take it off the grill and carefully wrap it up snugly in either aluminum foil or a butcher paper. Let it sit there for a good 30 minutes, giving those juices plenty of time to spread out.

9. After resting, unwrap the beef and place it on a large cutting board. Using two forks or meat claws, shred the beef into bite-sized pieces, discarding any large chunks of fat or gristle.

10. Serve the smoked pulled beef on its own, or piled onto hamburger buns or sandwich rolls. You can also mix it with your favorite barbecue sauce for extra flavor. Enjoy!

Note:

*   You can use the pulled beef in tacos, burritos, and nachos, or even as a topping for baked potatoes or salads, which are versatile and delicious meal options.

Smoked Beef Burgers

Ingredients:

For the Burgers:

* 1 ½ pounds ground beef (preferably 80/20 lean to fat ratio)
* 1 teaspoon garlic powder
* 1 teaspoon onion powder
* 1 teaspoon smoked paprika
* 1 teaspoon salt
* ½ teaspoon black pepper
* 4 hamburger buns
* Lettuce leaves, tomato slices, onion slices (for garnish)

For the BBQ Sauce:

* ½ cup ketchup
* 2 tablespoons brown sugar
* 1 tablespoon apple cider vinegar
* 1 tablespoon Worcestershire sauce
* 1 teaspoon smoked paprika
* ½ teaspoon garlic powder
* Salt and pepper to taste

Instructions:

1. Get your grill fired up to a nice, medium-high heat, somewhere between 375 to 400°F (about 190 to 204°C).

2. In a little saucepan, blend ketchup, brown sugar, apple cider vinegar, Worcestershire sauce, smoked paprika, salt, garlic powder, and pepper.

3. Just let that mix simmer over medium heat for like 5 to 7 minutes, giving it a stir now and then until it starts to get a bit thicker. Once it's reached that sweet spot, take it off the heat and stash it aside for later use.

4. Get a large mixing bowl and dump in the ground beef, onion powder, garlic powder, smoked paprika, salt, and pepper.

5. Split that seasoned beef into four even lumps and form them into patties, not too thin, not too thick, about ¾ of an inch.

6. Give each patty a little press in the middle with your thumb, just gently, so they don't puff up like balloons while cooking.

7. Lay those beef patties on the grill that you've already heated up. Close the lid and grill for 4-5 minutes on the first side.

8. Flip the burgers and brush them generously with the prepared BBQ sauce. Grill for an additional 4-5 minutes on the other side or until the internal temperature reaches 160°F (71°C) for medium doneness.

9. In the last minute of grilling, place the hamburger buns, cut side down, on the grill to lightly toast them.

10. Place a grilled beef patty on the bottom half of each toasted bun.

11. Top with lettuce leaves, tomato slices, onion slices, and any other desired toppings.

12. Spread additional BBQ sauce on the top half of each bun.

13. Place the top half of the bun over the toppings to complete the burgers.

14. Serve up those smoky beef burgers right away! You can even pair them with your go-to sides like potato salad, coleslaw, or baked beans.
15. Enjoy the smoky BBQ beef burgers with your friends and family!

Smoked Beef Ribs

Ingredients:

Beef Ribs:

* 2 racks of beef ribs (plate ribs or back ribs)

For the Rub:

* 1/4 cup coarse kosher salt

* 1/4 cup coarse black pepper

* 2 tablespoons paprika

* 2 tablespoons garlic powder

* 2 tablespoons onion powder

* 1 tablespoon brown sugar

* 1 teaspoon mustard powder

* Mix in 1 teaspoon of cayenne pepper (This ingredient is optional: for a bit of seasoning)

For the Mop Sauce (optional):

* 1 cup apple cider vinegar

* 1/2 cup apple juice

* 1/4 cup Worcestershire sauce

* 1/4 cup olive oil

Instructions:

1. Strip off the membrane from the underside of the ribs. This helps the rub spike and allows for more even cooking.
2. In a bowl, mix all the rubbed ingredients together.
3. Apply a thick layer of rub to every part of the ribs. Make sure they are evenly coated.
4. Preheat your pellet grill to a precise 225°F (107°C).
5. Lay the ribs flat on the grill, making sure the bones are facing downwards.
6. Hold the temperature at a consistent 225°F during smoking.
7. Smoke the ribs for 6-8 hours, aiming for the meat to reach 203°F (95°C) internally and achieve tenderness.
8. If you choose to use the mop sauce, mix all the ingredients together in a bowl.
9. Mop or spritz the ribs with the sauce every hour during the smoking process to keep them moist and add extra flavor.
10. Once the ribs are cooked, take them off the grill and give them 15-20 minutes to rest, so the juices can spread through the meat.
11. Slice between the bones and serve the ribs with your preferred barbecue sauce, if desired.

Tips:

Choosing Ribs:

* Plate ribs are meatier and generally preferred for smoking, but back ribs also work well.

Temperature Control:

* To ensure a consistent temperature and precise internal temperature readings, use a digital thermometer.

Braised Short Ribs

Ingredients:

Short Ribs:

* 4-6 pieces of bone-in beef short ribs, about 3 inches long (approx. 4-5 lbs)

For the Rub:

* 1 tablespoon kosher salt

* 1 tablespoon black pepper

* 1 tablespoon garlic powder

* 1 tablespoon onion powder

* 1 tablespoon paprika

* 1 teaspoon dried thyme

* 1 teaspoon dried rosemary

For Braising:

* 2 tablespoons olive oil

* 1 onion, chopped

* 2 carrots, chopped

* 2 celery stalks, chopped

* 4 cloves garlic, minced

* 2 cups beef broth

* 1 cup red wine (This is optional, and you can substitute it with some additional beef broth)

* 2 tablespoons tomato paste

* 2 bay leaves

* Salt and pepper to taste

Instructions:

1. Remove excess moisture from the short ribs by patting them dry with paper towels, ensuring the rub adheres effectively.
2. Create the rub by mixing salt, pepper, garlic powder, onion powder, paprika, thyme, and rosemary together in a small bowl.
3. Rub the mixture all over the short ribs, covering them evenly. Let them sit at room temperature for about 30 minutes while you prepare the grill.
4. Preheat your pellet grill to 250°F (121°C).
5. If your pellet grill has a direct flame option or a sear box, sear the short ribs on all sides until browned. This step adds flavor but can be skipped if your grill doesn't have this feature.
6. In a large cast iron pan (suitable for use on the grill), heat olive oil over medium-high heat.
7. Add chopped onion, carrots, and celery. Sauté until softened, about 5-7 minutes.
8. Pop in the minced garlic and cook until it's nice and fragrant.
9. Toss in the tomato paste and let it simmer for a minute or two.
10. Place the seared or unseared short ribs into the pan with the vegetables.
11. Toss in the beef broth and, if you want, a bit of red wine. The liquid should come halfway up the sides of the ribs; adjust the amount if necessary.

12. Stir in the bay leaves and add salt and pepper to taste.
13. Transfer the pan with the short ribs and braising liquid to the pellet grill.
14. Pop on the lid and let the short ribs braise until they're fall-apart tender, about 3-4 hours. Check periodically to ensure the liquid level is maintained; add more broth if needed.
15. Once the short ribs are tender, remove them from the grill.
16. Dish up the short ribs with the reduced sauce and some sides you love, like mashed potatoes or roasted veggies.

T-Bones

Ingredients:

* 2 T-bone steaks, about 1 to 1.5 inches thick (approximately 1 pound each)

* 1/4 cup olive oil

* 2 cloves garlic, minced

* 1 tablespoon fresh rosemary, chopped

* 1 tablespoon fresh thyme, chopped

* Salt and pepper, to taste

* Coarse kosher salt

* Freshly ground black pepper

* Optional: additional herbs like rosemary or thyme for garnish

Instructions:

1. If using a marinade, whisk together olive oil, minced garlic, chopped rosemary, chopped thyme, salt, and pepper in a bowl. Place the steaks in a shallow dish or in a zip-lock bag and drizzle the marinade over. Cover it up or seal it and put it in the fridge for at least an hour, or you can go up to 4 hours.

2. If you're not marinating them, give both sides of the steaks a good sprinkle of kosher salt and freshly ground black pepper.

3. Heat up your grill to high (about 450-500°F or 230-260°C). Clean the grill grates well and grease them up so nothing sticks.
4. Place the T-bone steaks on the hot grill grate.
5. For medium-rare, grill for about 4-5 minutes per side, flipping only once. Use the meat thermometer to check—it should hit about 130 to 135°F for medium-rare, adjust it if you want it cooked differently.
6. Don't squish your steaks with the spatula—you'll squeeze out all the juices, making them less juicy.
7. To achieve a cross-hatch pattern, rotate each steak 45 degrees halfway through grilling on each side.
8. Once they're cooked, remove the steaks from the grill and give them a rest on a cutting board or plate for 5-10 minutes.
9. Serve the T-bone steaks whole or slice them off the bone. Garnish with additional herbs if desired.

Meaty Chuck Short Ribs

Ingredients:

* 4-6 pieces of chuck short ribs, bone-in, approximately 3-4 lbs total

For the Rub:

* 1/4 cup kosher salt

* 1/4 cup black pepper, coarsely ground

* 2 tablespoons paprika

* 2 tablespoons garlic powder

* 2 tablespoons onion powder

* 1 tablespoon brown sugar

* Mix in 1 teaspoon of cayenne pepper (This ingredient is optional: for a bit of seasoning)

For the Braising Liquid (optional):

* 2 cups beef broth

* 1 cup red wine (This is optional, and you can substitute it with some additional beef broth)

* 2 tablespoons Worcestershire sauce

* 2 tablespoons soy sauce

* 4 cloves garlic, minced

* 2 bay leaves

Instructions:

1. If preferred, you can trim off any extra fat from the short ribs.
2. In a bowl, combine all the ingredients for the rub: black pepper, garlic powder, kosher salt, onion powder, brown sugar, paprika and cayenne pepper.
3. Rub the mixture all over the chuck short ribs, ensuring they are evenly coated. You can let them sit with the rub for about 30 minutes at room temperature while you prepare the grill.
4. Preheat your pellet grill to 250°F (120°C).
5. Place the seasoned chuck short ribs directly on the grill grates.
6. Close the lid and smoke the ribs for about 2-3 hours. This initial smoking period helps infuse the meat with a smoky flavor.
7. Put the lid or foil back on the pan and return it to the pellet grill.
8. Let the chuck short ribs simmer in the braising liquid at 250°F (120°C) for another 2-3 hours until the meat is tender and comes off the bone easily.
9. Take the pan away from the grill and let the short ribs rest, covered, for about 10-15 minutes.
10. Optionally, skim any fat from the braising liquid and serve the ribs with the reduced sauce.

Meat Loaf

Ingredients:

For the Meatloaf:

* 2 lbs ground beef (preferably a mix of lean and fatty ground beef)
* 1 cup breadcrumbs
* 1/2 cup milk
* 2 eggs
* 1 small onion, finely chopped
* 2 cloves garlic, minced
* 1/4 cup ketchup
* 2 tablespoons Worcestershire sauce
* 1 tablespoon Dijon mustard
* 1 teaspoon salt
* 1/2 teaspoon black pepper
* 1/2 teaspoon dried thyme
* 1/2 teaspoon dried oregano
* 1/2 teaspoon smoked paprika (optional)

For the Glaze:

* 1/2 cup ketchup
* 2 tablespoons brown sugar
* 1 tablespoon apple cider vinegar
* 1 teaspoon Dijon mustard

* Pinch of salt and black pepper

Instructions:

1. Preheat your pellet grill to 350°F (175°C).
2. Combine all the ingredients—ground beef, breadcrumbs, milk, eggs, chopped onion, minced garlic, ketchup, Worcestershire sauce, Dijon mustard, salt, black pepper, dried thyme, dried oregano, and smoked paprika (if you're adding it)—in a large bowl.
3. Mix everything together gently but thoroughly. Be careful not to overmix; you want the meatloaf to stay tender.
4. Press the meat mixture into a loaf shape on aluminum foil or a grill-safe pan. The loaf should be approximately 8 inches long and 4 inches wide.
5. Grill the meatloaf directly onto the grates or in a grill-safe pan.
6. Lower the lid on the pellet grill and cook at 350°F (175°C) for about an hour, or until it's reached 160°F (71°C) inside.
7. Blend together ketchup, brown sugar, apple cider vinegar, Dijon mustard, salt, and black pepper using a whisk.
8. About 15-20 minutes before the meatloaf is done, brush or spread the glaze evenly over the top of the meatloaf.
9. Close the lid and continue grilling for another 15-20 minutes, or until the glaze is caramelized and the internal temperature reaches 160°F (71°C).
10. Take the meatloaf off the grill and let it sit for 10 minutes before cutting.
11. Slice and serve the meatloaf with your favorite sides!

Roasted Whole Chicken

Ingredients:

* 1 whole chicken, about 4-5 pounds

* 2 tablespoons olive oil

* 1 tablespoon paprika

* 1 tablespoon garlic powder

* 1 tablespoon onion powder

* 1 teaspoon dried thyme

* 1 teaspoon dried rosemary

* 1 teaspoon dried oregano

* 1 teaspoon salt

* 1/2 teaspoon black pepper

* Fresh herbs for garnish. (Rosemary, parsley or thyme)

* Lemon slices or wedges for serving

Instructions:

1. Check for giblets inside the chicken cavity (if they're there) and use paper towels in order to dry the chicken.

2. You can truss the chicken (it's optional but a good idea) by wrapping its legs with kitchen twine and tucking the wings under.

3. Whisk olive oil with paprika, garlic powder, onion powder, dried rosemary, dried thyme, dried oregano, salt, and black pepper in a small bowl to make your rub.

4. Rub the chicken all over, including under the skin and inside the cavity, with the prepared rub mixture. Ensure it is evenly coated.

5. Preheat your pellet grill to 375°F (190°C).
6. Place the seasoned whole chicken directly on the grill grates, breast side up.
7. Pop the chicken on the grill and roast it for 1.5 to 2 hours, depending on its size and how well it cooks inside.
8. Insert the meat thermometer gently into the thickest and deepest part of the thigh (being careful not to go through the bone) to see if it's cooked through. It should register 165°F (74°C) internally.
9. If you prefer, baste the chicken with melted butter or olive oil every 30 minutes during the cooking process to keep it moist.
10. Once it's cooked, take the chicken off the grill and let it relax for 10-15 minutes before carving. This helps the juices move around and keeps the meat tender.
11. Break down the chicken into pieces and serve it with sides you love. Add some fresh herbs and lemon wedges for extra flavor if you want.

Smoke Whole Chicken

Ingredients:

* 1 whole chicken, about 4-5 pounds

For the Chicken Rub:

* 2 tablespoons olive oil or melted butter

* 1 tablespoon paprika

* 1 tablespoon garlic powder

* 1 tablespoon onion powder

* 1 teaspoon dried thyme

* 1 teaspoon dried rosemary

* 1 teaspoon dried oregano

* 1 teaspoon salt

* 1/2 teaspoon black pepper

Optional Brine (recommended for juicier meat):

* 4 cups water

* 1/4 cup salt

* 1/4 cup brown sugar

* Optional: herbs and spices of your choice (bay leaves, peppercorns, thyme, etc.)

Instructions:

1. Dissolve salt and brown sugar in water in a large bowl or container. Feel free to sprinkle in herbs and spices of your choice.

2. Soak the chicken in the brine, cover it up, and stick it in the fridge for 4 to 12 hours. Afterward, rinse it well with cold water and dab it dry with paper towels before you move on.
3. Grab the chicken from the brine (if you brined it) and gently pat it dry with paper towels.
4. Consider trussing the chicken—wrap twine around the legs and fold the wings under neatly.
5. Combine olive oil or melted butter with paprika, garlic powder, onion powder, dried thyme, rosemary, oregano, salt, and pepper in a small bowl. Use that as your rub.
6. Rub the chicken all over, including under the skin and inside the cavity, with the prepared rub mixture. Ensure it is evenly coated.
7. Preheat your pellet grill to 250°F (120°C).
8. Place the seasoned whole chicken directly on the grill grates, breast side up.
9. Close the lid of the pellet grill.
10. Smoke the chicken for roughly 2.5 to 3 hours until it's 165°F (74°C) in the thickest part of the thigh, checking with a meat thermometer as you go.
11. If you prefer, baste the chicken with melted butter or olive oil every hour during the smoking process to enhance flavor and keep the skin moist.
12. After cooking, take the chicken off the grill and give it a rest for about 10-15 minutes. This lets the juices settle for juicy, tender meat.
13. Then, carve it up and serve with your favorite sides. Sprinkle on some fresh herbs if desired.

Chicken Tenders

Ingredients:

* 1 pound chicken tenders (about 8-10 pieces)

* 1 cup buttermilk

* 1 cup all-purpose flour

* 1 teaspoon salt

* 1/2 teaspoon black pepper

* 1/2 teaspoon paprika

* 1/2 teaspoon garlic powder

* 1/2 teaspoon onion powder

* Cooking spray or oil for greasing the grill grates

Instructions:

1. Take the chicken tenders and dump them in a bowl. Pour buttermilk all over them, making sure they're fully covered. Let them cool in the fridge for at least 30 minutes, but you can also leave them in there for up to 4 hours. This makes the chicken nice, soft, and tender, giving it more flavor.
2. Get your pellet grill fired up to 375°F (190°C). Make sure the grill grates are clean, and give them a light coat of cooking spray or oil so that nothing sticks.
3. Mix the flour, salt, pepper, paprika, garlic powder, and onion powder in a dish or bowl until it's all blended.
4. Remove each chicken tender from the buttermilk marinade, allowing excess buttermilk to drip off. Dredge

each tender in the seasoned flour mixture, making sure they are all evenly coated. Press lightly to make sure that the flour sticks to the chicken.

5. Place the coated chicken tenders directly on the preheated grill grates. Close the grill lid and cook for about 5-7 minutes on each side. You'll know it's done when it's well-browned and reaches 165°F (74°C) inside.

6. After grilling, let the chicken tenders rest for a few minutes before serving them hot with your preferred dips or sides.

Buffalo Wings

Ingredients:

* 2-3 pounds chicken wings, cut into flats and drumettes

* 1/2 cup of hot sauce (Or your favorite Buffalo sauce)

* 1/4 cup unsalted butter, melted

* 1 tablespoon of honey (optional)

* 1 teaspoon garlic powder

* 1 teaspoon onion powder

* 1/2 teaspoon salt

* 1/2 teaspoon black pepper

* Cooking spray or oil for greasing the grill grates

Instructions:

1. Run those chicken wings under cold water, and dab them dry with paper towels. You can cut down any extra skin or fat if there's too much.

2. Combine the hot sauce, melted butter, onion powder, honey (if you want it sweeter), garlic powder, salt, and pepper in a bowl. Mix it well—that's your homemade Buffalo sauce right there.

3. Pop the chicken wings into a big bowl or a zip-top bag. Pour about half of the Buffalo sauce over the wings, reserving the rest for later. Give the wings a good toss to make sure they're coated all over.

4. Shove it in the fridge for at least an hour (or overnight) to let the flavors mix.

5. Warm up your pellet grill to 400°F (200°C). Spray or oil the grill grates so nothing gets stuck.

6. Place the marinated chicken wings on the preheated grill grates in a single layer. Drop the lid and grill for about 25-30 minutes, flipping halfway, until the wings are cooked through and crispy on the outside. See if it's hit 165°F (74°C) inside.

7. Remove the grilled wings from the grill and place them in a clean bowl. Pour the remaining Buffalo sauce over the wings and toss them gently to coat evenly.

8. Put the Buffalo wings on a platter and serve them hot with celery sticks and your favorite dip—blue cheese or ranch dressing.

Tips:

Crispiness: If you prefer extra crispy wings, you can increase the temperature slightly during the last few minutes of grilling or finish them under a broiler for a minute or two.

Lemon Pepper Chicken

Ingredients:

* 4 boneless, skinless chicken breasts

* 2 tablespoons olive oil

* 2 tablespoons lemon juice

* 2 teaspoons lemon zest

* 2 teaspoons black pepper (adjust to taste)

* 1 teaspoon salt (adjust to taste)

* 1 teaspoon garlic powder

* 1 teaspoon onion powder

* 1 teaspoon paprika (optional, for color)

* Fresh parsley, chopped (for garnish)

Instructions:

1. Wash the chicken breasts under cold water and dry them with paper towels.
2. Combine lemon juice, lemon zest, black pepper, salt, garlic powder, olive oil, onion powder, and paprika (if using) in a bowl.
3. Stick the chicken breasts in a zip-top bag or dish and pour on the marinade, making sure the chicken breasts are well-coated.
4. Cover it up with plastic wrap and keep it in the fridge for at least 30 minutes to marinate. For the tastiest outcome, shoot for 2 to 4 hours.

5. Preheat your pellet grill to 375°F (190°C) according to manufacturer instructions. If your pellet grill doesn't go this high, aim for the highest setting available.
6. Extract the chicken from the marinade and toss the leftover stuff.
7. Place the chicken breasts straight on the grill.
8. Cover it up and let it cook for 6 to 8 minutes on each side until the chicken reaches 165°F inside. Timing might change based on how thick your chicken is.
9. Take the chicken off the grill once it's cooked through, and let it rest for a few minutes before serving.
10. If you want, top it off with some freshly chopped parsley before serving.
11. Serve your lemon pepper chicken hot, accompanied by your favorite sides!

Smoked Drumsticks

Ingredients:

* 8-10 chicken drumsticks

* 2 tablespoons olive oil

* 2 tablespoons paprika

* 1 tablespoon garlic powder

* 1 tablespoon onion powder

* 1 tablespoon brown sugar

* 1 teaspoon salt

* 1 teaspoon black pepper

* Optional: your favorite BBQ sauce for brushing

Instructions:

1. Wash the drumsticks in cold water and then towel them dry.
2. Chuck them in a bowl.
3. Coat the drumsticks by drizzling olive oil over them and tossing gently.
4. Take a small bowl and mix some garlic powder, onion powder, brown sugar, paprika, black pepper, and salt.
5. Sprinkle the seasoning mixture over the drumsticks, tossing them again to ensure they are well coated with the spices.
6. Preheat your pellet grill to 225-250°F (107-121°C).
7. Arrange the seasoned drumsticks directly on the grill grate, leaving some space between each piece for the smoke to circulate.

8. Cover the lid and smoke the drumsticks for around 1.5 to 2 hours until they reach 165°F (74°C) inside.
9. If you like, you can brush the drumsticks with your favorite BBQ sauce at the end. Cook it like this to caramelize the sauce and get a sweet, sticky coating.
10. Once the drumsticks are done, remove them from the grill and let them rest for a few minutes before serving.
11. Enjoy your delicious smoked drumsticks!

Smoked Quarters

Ingredients:

* 4 chicken quarters (thigh and drumstick attached)
* Olive oil (for coating)

Dry Rub:

* 2 tablespoons paprika
* 1 tablespoon brown sugar
* 1 tablespoon garlic powder
* 1 tablespoon onion powder
* 1 tablespoon chili powder
* 1 teaspoon cumin
* 1 teaspoon dried thyme
* 1 teaspoon dried oregano
* 1 teaspoon salt
* 1/2 teaspoon black pepper
* Mix in 1 teaspoon of cayenne pepper (This ingredient is optional: for a bit of seasoning)

Brine (optional but recommended):

* 4 cups water
* 1/4 cup salt
* 1/4 cup brown sugar
* 2 cloves garlic (crushed)
* 1 bay leaf

*   1 teaspoon black peppercorns

Instructions:

If using the brine:

1. Mix water, salt, brown sugar, bay leaf, crushed garlic and black peppercorns in a large bowl.
2. Submerge the chicken quarters in the brine. Cover and refrigerate for 4-6 hours.
3. Once the brining's done, take the chicken quarters out of the brine, wash them in cold water, and dry them off with paper towels.

If not using the brine:

1. Lightly coat each chicken quarter with olive oil. This helps the dry rub adhere and also promotes a nice crispy skin.
2. Mix up all of the dry rub in a little bowl. Rub it all over the chicken quarters, making sure every part gets some. Let it sit for 15-30 minutes so the flavors sink in.
3. Preheat your pellet grill to 225°F (107°C). This low temperature allows the chicken to absorb maximum smoke flavor.
4. Arrange the chicken quarters on the grill grates, skin-side up. Close the lid.
5. Smoke the chicken at 225°F for around 2 to 2.5 hours, checking that the thickest part reaches 165°F (74°C).
6. If you prefer crispier skin, increase the temperature of the grill to 375°F (190°C) for the last 10-15 minutes of cooking.
7. Once the chicken quarters are done on the grill, let them sit there for 10 minutes.

8. Serve the smoked chicken quarters with your favorite sides, such as cornbread, coleslaw, or grilled vegetables.

94

Teriyaki Smoked Drumsticks

Ingredients:

* Chicken drumsticks

* Olive oil

* Salt

* Black pepper

* Garlic powder

* Teriyaki sauce (store-bought or homemade)

* Optional: Feel free to add a sprinkle of sesame seeds and green onions for garnish.

Instructions:

1. Dry off the chicken drumsticks with paper towels to help the seasoning and sauce cling.
2. Lightly brush the drumsticks with olive oil, then sprinkle with black pepper, salt and garlic powder.
3. Start your pellet grill and set it to smoke mode or a low temperature around 225-250°F (107-121°C). Pellet grills are perfect for smoking because they maintain a consistent temperature and add a nice smoky flavor.
4. Place the seasoned drumsticks directly on the grill grate once it's preheated. Close the lid and smoke the drumsticks for about 1.5 to 2 hours.
5. About 15-20 minutes before the drumsticks are done, brush them generously with teriyaki sauce. This lets the

sauce caramelize and form a sticky, tasty glaze. You can do this step multiple times for a thicker glaze.

6. After the drumsticks reach the desired internal temperature and are nicely glazed, remove them from the grill.

7. For a boost in flavor and presentation, top the drumsticks with some sesame seeds and chopped green onions before serving.

8. Serve your teriyaki smoked drumsticks hot and enjoy the combination of smoky flavor and sweet-savory teriyaki glaze!

Roasted Duck

Ingredients:

* Whole duck

* Salt and pepper

* Optional: herbs like thyme, rosemary, or sage for some seasoning

* Pellets for your pellet grill (choose a flavor that complements duck, like oak or cherry)

Instructions:

1. Start by prepping the duck. Remove any giblets you see and give it a good pat-down with paper towels.
2. Don't forget to give the duck a good seasoning inside and out with salt and pepper. You can also pop some herbs in the cavity for more taste.
3. Turn on your pellet grill and set the temperature to about 250-275°F (120-135°C). Give it a few minutes with the lid down to warm up.
4. Place the seasoned duck directly onto the grill grates breast-side up. Close the lid.
5. Let the duck cook for about 2-3 hours, depending on its size and the temperature of your grill. You can rotate the duck halfway through cooking for even browning.
6. Check the duck's doneness with a meat thermometer—ensure that the thigh hits 165°F (74°C) at its thickest point.
7. Once the duck's cooked, take it off the grill and give it about 10-15 minutes before carving.

8. Cut the duck into portions and pair it with sides and sauces you like.

Smoked Turkey

Ingredients:

* A whole turkey, fresh or unfrozen after thawing

* Salt and pepper

* Olive oil or use melted butter (This step is optional: for basting)

Instructions:

1. Pull the turkey out of the package and towel it off to dry it. Season it well inside and out with salt and pepper, and you can also season under the skin for added yum.
2. Optional: Give the turkey's outer skin a rubdown with olive oil or melted butter to crisp it up.
3. Turn on your pellet grill and set the temperature to smoke mode or around 225-250°F (107-121°C).
4. Chuck the seasoned turkey on the grill grates, making sure the breast side is up. If your pellet grill has a temperature probe, insert it into the thickest part of the breast or thigh.
5. Seal the lid and let the turkey smoke for several hours. The time it takes varies based on the turkey's size and how hot your grill is. As a general guide, plan for about 30-40 minutes per pound of turkey.
6. To achieve moist skin and uniform browning, you could baste the turkey with olive oil or melted butter every 1-2 hours, if that's your preference.
7. Pop a meat thermometer into the turkey's thigh—it needs to reach 165°F (74°C) without touching the bone.

8. Once the turkey reaches the perfect temperature, carefully pull it off the grill and cover it loosely with foil. Give it a good 20-30 minutes to rest before slicing.
9. Carve the smoked turkey into slices and arrange on a serving platter.
10. Pair it with your go-to sides and enjoy the delicious smoky taste!

Tips:

*   Ensure your pellet grill is well-maintained and clean before starting to ensure optimal smoking performance.

*   Consider adding aromatics like garlic, herbs, or citrus inside the cavity of the turkey for extra flavor and taste.

Roast Turkey

Ingredients:

* A whole turkey, fresh or unfrozen after thawing

* Salt and pepper

* Olive oil or melted butter

* Fresh herbs (optional, such as thyme, rosemary, and sage)

Instructions:

* Grab the turkey out of the packaging and dry it off using paper towels.

* Preheat your pellet grill to around 325-350°F (163-177°C), using the appropriate setting according to your grill's instructions.

* Rub the outside of the turkey generously with olive oil or melted butter.

* Coat the turkey fully inside and out with salt and pepper. If desired, you can also place fresh herbs like thyme, rosemary, and sage inside the cavity for additional flavor.

* Flip that seasoned turkey onto the grill, breast up facing up.

* Pop the grill lid down and let the turkey roast. Cooking time varies, but plan on 13-15 minutes per pound at 325-350°F (163-177°C).

* Make sure you're watching the turkey's temp with a meat thermometer. Once it hits 165°F (74°C), it's cooked.

* Once your turkey's cooked enough, pull it off the pellet grill and onto a cutting board.

* Wrap the turkey loosely in foil and leave it be for 20-30 minutes.

* Slice up the turkey and present it in a delightful arrangement on a platter.

* Serve the roasted turkey with your favorite sides and garnishes.

Buttered Thanksgiving Turkey

Ingredients:

* A whole turkey, fresh or unfrozen after thawing

* Salt and pepper

* Butter (softened)

* Fresh herbs (optional, such as thyme, rosemary, and sage)

* Garlic cloves (optional, for additional flavor)

Instructions:

1. Take the turkey out of the packaging and blot it dry with some damp paper towels. Then, fire up your pellet grill and get it preheated to about 325-350°F (163-177°C), following the grill's instructions.
2. Give the turkey a good, hefty dose of salt and pepper, both inside and out.
3. In a little bowl, blend softened butter with chopped fresh herbs (if you've got them). Drop in a bit of minced garlic to jazz it up.
4. Gently peel back the turkey skin and slide some of the butter mix in there. It will make sure the meat stays moist and tastes great.
5. Take what's left of the butter mix and rub it all over the turkey's outside, covering it evenly.
6. Slide the buttered turkey onto the grill grates of the pellet grill, with the breast side facing up.

7. Close the grill lid and let the turkey roast up. For cooking time, figure about 13-15 minutes per pound at 325-350°F (163-177°C), adjusting for the turkey's size.
8. Keep the turkey moist and tasty by occasionally spooning it with the pan drippings or adding more melted butter.
9. Poke the thermometer into the plumpest part of the thigh; keep it away from the bone. Once it reads 165°F (74°C), it's safe to eat!
10. After the turkey reaches the target temperature, safely remove it from the pellet grill and transfer it to a cutting board.
11. Give the turkey a foil cape and let it hang out for a good 20-30 minutes.
12. Cut the turkey into slices and arrange them neatly on a fancy platter.
13. Serve the buttered Thanksgiving turkey with your favorite sides, such as stuffing, cranberry sauce, and roasted vegetables. Enjoy!

Smoked Turkey Breast

Ingredients:

* Turkey breast (bone-in or boneless)

* Olive oil or melted butter

* Salt and pepper

* Any seasoning you like (maybe a spice rub or herbs)

Instructions:

1. To begin, dry off the turkey breast with some damp paper towels. It makes the spices stick really well!

2. Spread the turkey breast well with some olive oil or melted butter. It adds a unique flavor and helps achieve that perfect crispy skin.

3. Give the turkey breast a good, gentle sprinkling of salt and pepper, and if you've got a favorite spice mix, go ahead and dust that on both sides evenly.

4. Fire up your pellet grill and set it to smoke at around 225-250°F (107-121°C). This low heat cooks the turkey breast slowly, letting it soak in that smoky goodness.

5. Place your well-seasoned turkey breast directly on the hot grill grates of the pellet grill.

6. Close the lid securely and let it slowly smoke away. It should be ready in around 2.5 to 3 hours, but keep an eye on it, especially if your grill runs hot or the breast is on the larger side.

7. Poke the thermometer into the turkey breast's deepest spot to make sure it's cooked all the way through. You're

looking for it to hit 165°F (74°C) to make sure it's cooked through and safe to eat.

8. Once it's reached the right temperature, take the turkey breast off the grill and let it rest for about 10-15 minutes. This step helps the flavors blend and keeps the meat nice and delicate.

9. Slice it up against the grain, plate it with your favorite sides, and dig in!

Smoked Turkey Wings

Ingredients:

* Turkey wings (fresh)
* Olive oil or melted butter
* Salt and pepper
* Your favorite seasoning blend or dry rub

Instructions:

1. Before seasoning, give the turkey wings a quick pat-down with some paper towels. It will help keep the seasoning on and make them nice and crunchy!
2. Brush the wings all over with olive oil or melted butter. It adds flavor and makes it turn all golden brown!
3. Carefully sprinkle those turkey wings with flavorful salt and cracked black pepper, ensuring every bit is perfectly seasoned. If you have a favorite dry rub or seasoning blend, sprinkle that on too. Coat them evenly for maximum flavor.
4. Get your pellet grill fired up and set it to smoke mode or a low temperature around 225-250°F (107-121°C). This slow-cooking method lets the wings absorb that delicious smokiness.
5. Place your seasoned turkey wings directly on the grill grates of the pellet grill.
6. Close the lid and let them smoke away. It usually takes about 2 to 2.5 hours, but keep an eye on them to make sure they're cooking evenly.
7. Slide a meat thermometer into the plumpest and chunkiest part of the turkey wings. The temperature inside should precisely hit 165°F (74°C) to ensure the turkey wings are completely done and perfectly safe to enjoy.
8. Once they're done, take the smoked turkey wings off the grill and let them rest for a few minutes. This helps the juices settle and keeps them tender.
9. Get ready to enjoy them hot and crispy with your favorite sauce or as a yummy snack!

Shrimp Scampi

Ingredients:

* 1 pound of large shrimp (It should be peeled and deveined)

* 4 tablespoons butter

* 4 cloves garlic, minced

* 1/4 cup of white wine (optional, chicken broth is a good substitute)

* 1 tablespoon lemon juice

* 1 teaspoon lemon zest

* 1/4 teaspoon of red pepper flakes (Adding red pepper is optional—if you like it spicy)

* Salt and pepper to taste

* 2 tablespoons fresh parsley, chopped

* Perfect with cooked pasta or alongside crusty bread (for serving)

Instructions:

1. Heat your pellet grill to 350°F (175°C). While it's preheating, season the shrimp in a large bowl with salt, pepper, and red pepper flakes.
2. Place a cast-iron skillet or grill-safe pan on the grill.
3. Get the butter melted and toss in the minced garlic. Cook it for a couple of minutes until it smells great and starts to get soft.

4. Lay the shrimp out in the skillet, making sure they're in a single layer.
5. Let them cook for a few minutes per side until they turn rosy pink and firm. Then, add in the white wine (or chicken broth) and lemon juice.
6. Add some lemon zest to the mix.
7. Stir everything together and let it cook for another 2-3 minutes until the sauce slightly reduces.
8. Sprinkle some finely chopped parsley over the shrimp.
9. Taste the rich flavor and add some extra salt, freshly ground pepper, or tangy lemon juice to your liking.
10. Plate it up immediately over cooked pasta or with some crusty bread.
11. Enjoy your scrumptious shrimp scampi right off the grill!

Barbecued Shrimp

Ingredients:

* 1 pound of large shrimp (It should be peeled and deveined)
* 2 tablespoons olive oil
* 2 cloves garlic, minced
* 1 teaspoon paprika
* 1/2 teaspoon cayenne pepper (adjust to taste)
* 1/2 teaspoon onion powder
* 1/2 teaspoon dried thyme
* 1/2 teaspoon dried oregano
* Salt and pepper to taste
* Optional: top it off with 2 tablespoons of fresh parsley, chopped.
* Lemon wedges, for serving

Instructions:

1. Get your pellet grill nice and hot, aiming for around 375-400°F (190-200°C).
2. For the marinade, mix olive oil, paprika, minced garlic, cayenne pepper, dried thyme, dried oregano, salt, and pepper and onion powder in a bowl.
3. Make sure the peeled and deveined shrimp are well coated with the marinade by tossing them together.

4. If you're opting for wooden skewers, then soak them in water for roughly 30 minutes to avoid them getting charred.
5. Put the marinated shrimp onto skewers, spacing them evenly along the way.
6. Position the shrimp skewers on the grill that's already preheated.
7. Grill for 2-3 minutes per side or until the shrimp are opaque and slightly charred, brushing with any remaining marinade while grilling.
8. Grab the shrimp skewers off the grill once they're ready.
9. For a touch of freshness, sprinkle with chopped parsley if you want, and serve with lemon wedges on the side.

Tip:

* Serve barbecued shrimp as an appetizer or serve it as part of a main course with sides like rice, salad, or grilled vegetables.

Smoked Salmon

Ingredients:

* 1 pound (about 450g) salmon fillet, preferably with skin on
* Measure out 1/4 cup of kosher salt (or sea salt).
* 1/4 cup brown sugar
* 1 tablespoon freshly ground black pepper
* Lemon wedges, for serving (optional)
* Dill sprigs, for garnish (optional)

Instructions:

1. Wash the salmon fillet under cold water and then dry it with paper towels. Check for bones and remove them if you spot any.
2. Combine brown sugar, kosher salt, and black pepper in a bowl to make the curing mixture.
3. Lay a big sheet of plastic wrap or aluminum foil on your clean work area.
4. Spread half of the curing mixture evenly over the wrap in a shape slightly larger than the salmon fillet.
5. Lay the salmon fillet, skin-side down, on top of the curing mixture.
6. Sprinkle all the remaining flavorful curing mixture evenly over the top and around the salmon.
7. Make sure the salmon is snugly wrapped in the plastic wrap or foil, sealing it well.
8. Place the wrapped salmon into a wide dish or baking pan to catch any excess liquid that might spill out during curing.
9. Refrigerate for 12-24 hours. Letting it cure longer will make the salmon saltier and firmer.
10. Before smoking, wash the cured salmon under cold water to get rid of the curing mixture.
11. Preheat your pallet grill to a low temperature, ideally around 175-200°F (80-95°C).
12. If your pallet grill has a water pan, fill it with water to help maintain moisture.
13. Place the salmon fillet directly on the grill grate of the pellet grill, skin-side down.
14. Smoke the salmon for 1.5 to 2 hours, or until it reaches up to 145°F (63°C) inside and flakes easily with a fork.

15. Once smoked, carefully remove the salmon from the pallet grill and let it cool to room temperature.
16. Optionally, refrigerate the smoked salmon for a few hours before serving to enhance the flavors.
17. Serve smoked salmon chilled or at room temperature.
18. Sprinkle on some lemon wedges and dill sprigs (for garnish).
19. Enjoy as an appetizer, on a bagel with cream cheese, or as part of a charcuterie board.

Tip:

*   Choose fresh, top-quality salmon for the best results.

Grilled Salmon

Ingredients:

* 4 Salmon fillets

* Olive oil

* Lemon juice

* Salt

* Pepper

* Optional: herbs like dill, thyme, or rosemary for seasoning

Instructions:

1. Get your pellet grill going at a medium-high heat, around 375-400°F (190-200°C). It's perfect for salmon with its steady temperature control.
2. Blot the salmon fillets with paper towels so the seasoning stays on.
3. Put olive oil on both sides of the salmon fillets and spread it all over with your hands.
4. Put just a touch of salt and pepper on the salmon fillet to make it delicious. You can also add herbs or a little lemon juice if you want it to taste even better.
5. Lay the salmon fillets directly on the grill grates, skin side down.
6. Drop the lid and let the salmon cook for 6-8 minutes per side, depending on how thick the fillets are. It's roughly 10 minutes per inch thick; just flip it once in the middle.

7. Poke it lightly with a fork to see if the salmon flakes easily and reaches 145°F (63°C) inside. Keep it moist by not cooking it too much.
8. When it's ready, use a spatula to take the salmon off the grill. Serve it right away with sides like salad, grilled veggies, or rice.

Lobster Tail

Ingredients:

* 4 lobster tails (either fresh or thawed from the freezer)

* 1/2 cup butter, melted

* 2 cloves garlic, minced (optional)

* Juice of 1 lemon

* Salt

* Pepper

* Optional: If you're feeling fancy, chop up some fresh parsley or chives to sprinkle over the top

Instructions:

1. Fire up your pellet grill to around 400°F (200°C) — that's the sweet spot for cooking seafood. It'll give your dish that perfect, even heat and just a touch of smokiness.

2. Grab some kitchen shears and cut down the top shell of each lobster tail lengthwise, right down the middle. Just be sure not to slice through the bottom shell or the meat inside.

3. Gently crack open the shell and lift the lobster meat, making sure it stays connected at the bottom. Then, just lay the meat on top of the shell.

4. Mix up melted butter, minced garlic (if you're feeling fancy), lemon juice, salt, and pepper in a small bowl. Give that lobster meat a nice, generous brush-down with this flavorful blend.

5. Simply place the prepped lobster tails on the grill grates, ensuring the meat side is facing upwards.

6. Pop the lid down and cook the lobster tails for about 8-10 minutes until the meat becomes fully cooked, gets a bit golden, and reaches 140-145°F (60-63°C) inside.
7. Lift the lobster tails off the grill with tongs or a spatula, taking care not to drop them. You can finish them off with some fresh herbs if you like.
8. Serve immediately with additional melted butter or lemon wedges on the side for dipping. Enjoy!

Smoked Trout

Ingredients:

* Whole trout or trout fillets

* Salt

* Pepper

* Olive oil

* Optional: lemon slices, fresh herbs (like thyme or dill) for seasoning

Instructions:

1. Get your pellet grill heating up nice and low, around 180-200°F (80-95°C). This slow-cooking trick is spot-on for smoking fish.
2. After that, give the trout a good pat-down with paper towels. It sets the stage for perfect seasoning.
3. Give both sides of the trout a light brush with olive oil. It'll make sure it doesn't stick and gives it an extra flavor boost.
4. Sprinkle the trout with salt and pepper as you prefer. To make it extra special, place thin lemon slices and fragrant fresh herbs inside the cavity of the whole trout.
5. Place the seasoned trout directly onto the grill grates, ensuring there is space between each piece for smoke circulation.
6. Pop the lid down on the pellet grill and let the trout smoke away for about 1.5 to 2 hours, or until it reaches 145°F (63°C) inside. The exact cooking duration varies based on the size and width of your trout.

7. Don't forget to peek at the pellet grill every now and then to keep that temperature in the sweet spot. It's key for smoking fish to get that perfect, consistent heat.
8. Once your trout's perfectly smoked, scoop it off the grill nice and easy with a spatula. Serve it up hot or cold, depending on what tickles your taste buds!
9. Enjoy smoked trout with crackers, a light salad, or simply as a standalone dish.

Smoked Rabbit

Ingredients:

* Whole rabbit, cleaned and quartered

* Olive oil

* Salt, to taste

* Pepper, to taste

* 1 teaspoon garlic powder

* 1 teaspoon onion powder

* 1 teaspoon paprika

* Season with aromatic herbs such as thyme or rosemary (Optional)

Instructions:

1. Get your pellet grill nice and toasty at a low temperature, around 225-250°F (107-121°C). This slow cooking will let that rabbit soak up all that smoky goodness.
2. Dry off those rabbit pieces with paper towels to ensure they're moisture-free. Then, coat them in olive oil to make sure the seasoning holds tight.
3. Take a small bowl and whip up a mix of garlic powder, paprika, salt, pepper, and onion powder. Give those rabbit pieces a nice dusting with this spice blend, making sure to cover them all around. Don't forget, tossing in some fresh herbs can really uplift the flavor!
4. Place the seasoned rabbit pieces directly onto the grill grates, ensuring there is space between each piece for smoke circulation.

5. Drop the lid on the pellet grill and let the rabbit smoke for about 2.5 to 3 hours. How long it smokes depends on the rabbit piece size and your grill heat. Ensure it hits 160°F (71°C) inside for a delicious and safe meal.
6. Once your rabbit is smoked to your liking and reaches that perfect texture, carefully take it off the grill with tongs or a spatula.
7. Allow it to rest briefly before serving. Enjoy it hot alongside your favorite sides, like roasted veggies, potatoes, or a refreshing salad.

Smoked Duck

Ingredients:

* Whole duck

* Salt

* Pepper

* Your favorite duck rub or seasoning (optional)

Instructions:

1. Before you smoke the duck, make sure to rinse it thoroughly under cold water.
2. After that, gently pat it dry with paper towels. When you trim off any extra fat, be careful to leave a thin layer to keep the meat juicy while it smokes.
3. Don't skimp on the seasoning—give the duck a good coating of salt, pepper, and any additional seasoning or rub you like, including inside the cavity.
4. Preheat the grill to a temperature range of 225 to 250°F (107-121°C). This gentle, prolonged cooking process ensures the duck cooks evenly while absorbing the rich, smoky flavors.
5. Just stick the seasoned duck on the grill grates, with the breast side up.
6. Flip the lid shut on the pellet grill and let the duck get its smoky flavor for about 3 to 4 hours, or until it reaches up to 165°F (74°C) inside. Keep an eye on it—timing depends on the duck's size and your grill's heat.

7. Feel free to give the duck a baste with its own juices or a light glaze every hour—it'll enhance the flavor and keep it nice and pulpy.
8. Keep smoking the duck and check every 30 minutes until it's cooked to perfection.
9. When it's finished cooking, take the duck off the grill and let it sit for 10-15 minutes so it's not too hot when you start slicing.
10. Slice up the smoky duck and serve it while it's still warm. It goes great with sides like roasted veggies, rice, or a fresh salad.

Smoked Alligator

Ingredients:

* Alligator meat (typically tail meat or ribs)

* Salt

* Pepper

* Your favorite Cajun or barbecue seasoning

* Olive oil or cooking oil spray (optional, for coating)

Instructions:

1. If you're working with a whole alligator tail or ribs, give them a good clean and cut off any extra fat or tough bits. Alligator meat's pretty lean, so a bit of fat keeps it nice and juicy as it smokes.

2. Cut the alligator meat into manageable pieces or ribs if needed.

3. Sprinkle salt, pepper, and your preferred Cajun or barbecue seasoning generously over the alligator pieces. Make sure to get seasoning on all sides evenly, and a touch of olive oil or cooking spray can help keep it in place.

4. Warm up the grill to a low temperature, around 225-250°F (107-121°C). Slow cooking like this is excellent for smoking alligator, letting it take in the smoky flavor throughout.

5. Lay the seasoned alligator pieces right on the grill grates. Spread them out so they're not packed tight, letting the smoke swirl around each piece.

6. Flip down the pellet grill lid and let the alligator smoke for about 2-3 hours, or until it reaches up to 145°F (63°C) inside.

7. Keep an eye on the alligator pieces as they smoke. About halfway through, it might be a good idea to brush them with a light glaze or marinade to enhance their flavor and retain moisture.

8. When the smoked alligator is done just right, take it off the grill and give it a short rest before serving.

9. Plate it hot and serve with your go-to sides. Smoked alligator goes perfectly with Cajun-style rice, grilled veggies, or a crisp salad.

Smoked Venison

Ingredients:

* Venison (deer meat), preferably a cut like a roast or tenderloin
* Salt and pepper to taste (or your go-to seasonings)

Instructions:

1. Start by preheating your pellet grill to a temperature around 225-250°F (107-121°C).
2. Hit the venison with a solid dose of salt and pepper, or rub it down with your go-to spices. Make sure it's all covered.
3. Position the seasoned venison on the grill grate.
4. Cover it up and let it smoke. Smaller pieces might need 1 to 2 hours, while bigger roasts could take 4 hours or even more.
5. During the smoking process, periodically check the internal temperature of the venison using a meat thermometer. To get a medium-rare steak, aim for 135°F (57°C) and for a solid medium, go with 145°F (63°C).
6. When the venison is done the way you like, take it off the grill and let it rest for about 10-15 minutes.
7. Cut the smoked venison against the grain into thin slices. Serve it hot with your go-to sides, such as roasted vegetables or a fresh salad.